THE LIGHT OF WISDOM, VOL. III

TEACHINGS ON THE SECRET EMPOWERMENT

RANGJUNG YESHE BOOKS • *www.rangjung.com*

PADMASAMBHAVA: *Treasures from Juniper Ridge* •
Advice from the Lotus-Born • *Dakini Teachings* •
Following in Your Footsteps: The Lotus-Born Guru in Nepal •
Following in Your Footsteps: The Lotus-Born Guru in India

PADMASAMBHAVA AND JAMGÖN KONGTRÜL:
The Light of Wisdom, Vol. 1, Vol. 2, Vol. 3, Secret, Vol. 4 & Vol. 5

PADMASAMBHAVA, CHOKGYUR LINGPA, JAMYANG KHYENTSE WANGPO,
TULKU URGYEN RINPOCHE, ORGYEN TOBGYAL RINPOCHE, & OTHERS
Dispeller of Obstacles • *The Tara Compendium* • *Powerful Transformation* •
Dakini Activity

YESHE TSOGYAL: *The Lotus-Born*

DAKPO TASHI NAMGYAL: *Clarifying the Natural State*

TSELE NATSOK RANGDRÖL: *Mirror of Mindfulness* • *Heart Lamp*

CHOKGYUR LINGPA: *Ocean of Amrita* • *The Great Gate* • *Skillful Grace* •
Great Accomplishment • *Guru Heart Practices*

TRAKTUNG DUDJOM LINGPA: *A Clear Mirror*

JAMGÖN MIPHAM RINPOCHE:
Gateway to Knowledge, Vol. 1, Vol. 2, Vol. 3, & Vol. 4

TULKU URGYEN RINPOCHE: *Blazing Splendor* • *Rainbow Painting* •
As It Is, Vol. 1 & Vol. 2 • *Vajra Speech* • *Repeating the Words of the Buddha* •
Dzogchen Deity Practice • *Vajra Heart Revisited*

ADEU RINPOCHE: *Freedom in Bondage*

KHENCHEN THRANGU RINPOCHE: *Crystal Clear*

CHÖKYI NYIMA RINPOCHE: *Bardo Guidebook* •
Collected Works of Chökyi Nyima Rinpoche, Vol. 1 & Vol. 2

TULKU THONDUP: *Enlightened Living*

ORGYEN TOBGYAL RINPOCHE: *Life & Teachings of Chokgyur Lingpa* •
Straight Talk • *Sublime Lady of Immortality*

DZIGAR KONGTRÜL RINPOCHE: *Uncommon Happiness*

TSOKNYI RINPOCHE: *Fearless Simplicity* • *Carefree Dignity*

MARCIA BINDER SCHMIDT: *Dzogchen Primer* • *Dzogchen Essentials* •
Quintessential Dzogchen • *Confessions of a Gypsy Yogini* •
Precious Songs of Awakening Compilation

ERIK PEMA KUNSANG: *Wellsprings of the Great Perfection* •
A Tibetan Buddhist Companion • *The Rangjung Yeshe Tibetan-English
Dictionary of Buddhist Culture & Perfect Clarity*

THE LIGHT OF WISDOM, VOL. III

THE ROOT TEXT

Lamrim Yeshe Nyingpo

BY PADMASAMBHAVA

As recorded by Yeshe Tsogyal *and revealed and decoded by*
Jamyang Khyentse Wangpo *and* Chokgyur Lingpa

THE COMMENTARY

The Light of Wisdom

BY JAMGÖN KONGTRÜL THE FIRST

THE NOTES

Entering the Path of Wisdom

BY JAMYANG DRAKPA

As recorded by Jokyab Rinpoche

Supplemented with clarifying remarks by
Kyabje Dilgo Khyentse
and Kyabje Tulku Urgyen Rinpoche

Translated from the Tibetan
by Erik Pema Kunsang *with* Gyurme Avertin, Cortland Dahl,
Lopon Damchoe Wangmo, *and* Marcia Schmidt

Rangjung Yeshe Publications
Boudhanath, Hong Kong & Esby

Rangjung Yeshe Publications

Address letters to:
Rangjung Yeshe Publications
P.O. Box 395
Leggett, CA USA

First edition 1986
First published edition 2012
Printed in the United States of America

1 3 5 7 9 8 6 4 2

Publication Data:

The root text, Lamrim Yeshe Nyingpo, by Padmasambhava, as recorded by Yeshe
Tsogyal, and revealed and decoded by Jamyang Khyentse Wangpo and Chokgyur
Lingpa. The commentary, The Light of Wisdom, by Jamgön Kongtrül the First.
The notes, Entering The Path of Wisdom, by Jamyang Drakpa, as recorded by
Jokyab Rinpoche. Translated from the Tibetan by Erik Pema Kunsang
(Erik Hein Schmidt), Gyurme Avertin, Lopon Damchoe Wangmo,
and Marcia Binder Schmidt.

*The Root Text: bla ma'i thugs sgrub rdo rje drag rtsal las zhal gdams
lam rim ye shes snying po pad ma sam bha'i snying thig go.
The Commentary: bla ma'i thugs sgrub rdo rje drag rtsal las, zhal gdams
lam rim ye shes snying po'i 'grel pa ye shes snang ba rab tu rgyas pa.
The Notes: bla med nang rgyud sde gsum gyi rgyab chos pad-ma'i zhal gdams
lam rim ye snying 'grel pa ye shes snang ba'i zur rgyan brgyud ldan
bla ma'i zhal rgyun rnams brjed byang gcig bsdus ye shes lam 'jug.*

ISBN 978-0-9909978-5-6

1. The Light of Wisdom, Vol. III. 2. Eastern philosophy — Buddhism.
3. Vajrayana — Tibet. I. Title.

CONTENTS

EDITOR'S PREFACE

This final, public section of *The Light of Wisdom, Volume III: Teachings on the Secret Empowerment,* is once again a compilation of three texts: (1) *Lamrim Yeshe Nyingpo* (*The Gradual Path of the Wisdom Essence*), a terma root text recorded by Yeshe Tsogyal and revealed in unison by Chokgyur Lingpa and Jamyang Khyentse Wangpo; (2) *The Light of Wisdom,* a commentary on the *Lamrim Yeshe Nyingpo* by Jamgön Kongtrül the Great; (3) *Entering the Path of Wisdom,* notes on these teachings collected by Jokyab Rinpoche.

This material was not included in the previous book, *The Light of Wisdom: The Conclusion,* due to uncertainty and hesitation on my part because such teachings on *tsa lung* practice, channels, wind-energies, and essences (*bindus*) is kept secret, like the name of the empowerment itself that authorizes the practitioner to engage in these trainings. After reviewing the material and discussing with one of my teachers, both of us fully aware of the constraints, I felt it best to share this volume with sincere Western practitioners who will need and benefit from these teachings.

There are still restricted sections of these three works that are available with a lot of effort. However, it is my wish to fulfill the vajra command of Kyabje Dilgo Khyentse Rinpoche to Erik Pema Kunsang to translate the entire thing. So, here you have almost all of it.

As with all Rangjung Yeshe publications, this is a group effort: Sincere thanks go to all the translators—Erik Pema Kunsang, Gyurme Avertin, and Lopon Damchoe Wangmo; Meghan Howard, who agreed to edit even in the midst of motherhood and preparing her thesis; the proofreaders, Lynn Schroeder and Michael Yockey; the typesetter, Joan Olson; the beautiful cover designer, Kelly Roberts, for the beautiful cover; and any and all sponsors who patiently awaited and supported this project. As an aside, please understand that the notes by Jokyab Rinpoche were an unusual challenge, some were out of place, others incomplete, and one in particular, was extremely difficult to read. I am amazed at the perseverance of our team for completing them at all!

Finally, I am still in awe of this sublime material and the responsibility to offer it, which I take very seriously. Please forgive any errors and hold this volume with joy and love. To connect with these teachings is an accumulation of incredible merit from the past and positive aspirations. May it be a vibrant support for realization and accomplishment!

INTRODUCTION

ORGYEN TOBGYAL RINPOCHE

The path of the vase empowerment is for the practice of the development stage. The path of the secret empowerment is for the practices of channels, winds, and essences and mantra recitation. The path of the wisdom-knowledge empowerment is the practice of the emptiness of the example wisdom that leads the ultimate wisdom being to arise in your experience. The secret empowerment and the wisdom-knowledge empowerments are the completion stage with and without characteristics. The precious word empowerment authorizes you to practice *Dzogchen*, primordially pure *trekchö* and spontaneously present *tögal*.

The secret empowerment concerns practices for gaining control over the empty aspect. The key point for this is familiarity with the practices of channels, winds, and essences. If you are completely untrained with *tsa lung*, you will not be able to do vase breathing. Generally, the main point of development *Mahayoga* practice, the instructions connected to the vase empowerment, is visualizing the deity. The second empowerment, the secret empowerment, is *Anu Yoga* practice, the instructions connected to *tsa lung*. From the first, you need to know how to do the vase breathing. Of this there are three types: superior vase breathing; middling vase breathing; and the lowest form of vase breathing, the lesser. Setting aside the first two, if you cannot even do the lesser form of vase breathing, there is no way you will be able to do this practice.

Since these empowerments are connected to trainings, and if you want to practice by merging yourself with the four empowerments, you need to do tsa lung practice. If you have no familiarity with tsa lung practice, there is no point in going into the more elaborate aspects of this path.

During empowerments, like the *Chetsun Nyingtik,* there is mention of students visualizing the three channels and the four chakras, and the students need to know what is being talked about. If the student does not, it is not all right; one of the main important points of Vajrayana is missing. Also in the *Yumkha,* if you do not know tsa lung, you will not be able to practice it. The *Yumkha* has to do with your own body mandala.[1]

The examples for tsa lung practice are that the body is like a country. The channels are like the roads. The wind-energies are like a wild blind horse, and the mind is like a person. The body should be placed in the seven-point posture of Vairochana, and when that is done there is happiness in the country. When in this posture, some of the channels are blocked because the legs are in the full lotus posture. This is a cause for comfort in traveling "the roads." If the channels are correctly placed, then inwardly the wind-energies will be as well. Right now, the wind is like a wild blind horse. The wild blind horse runs around and cannot determine where to go; this is the example of the wind-energies in the body that just move anywhere. On the horse of the wind-energy rides the mind, which is like a crippled man who has no power to decide where to travel. That is how we ordinary people are. If you practice tsa lung, the body and the wind-energies become mastered and the mind becomes trained. If the wind is controlled, then you can direct the horse and the mind will do whatever you think of.

These are the three main channels. Imagine your body to be empty. From the top of your head, down to the secret place, is the central channel, the width of a finger. It is like a pillar in the middle of an empty house. At the top, it reaches to the open aperture of Brahma. It is called the central channel because it is in the middle of the body. It also has many names, like *kadarma.* Inside flow the wind-energies, like prayer flags blowing in the wind. To the right is the red *kyangma* channel, and to the left the blue *roma* channel. They bend forward at the top of the head, connecting with the two nostrils, and go down and meet the central channel at the navel. The diameters of these three channels are equal. The roma is not used and is like a corpse. The kyangma means the eunuch, because it is standing in a way like no other channels.

There are four chakras:[1] At the top of the head is *the great bliss chakra,* which has thirty-two spokes and faces downward like an open umbrella. The bliss of *bodhichitta* is formed in the head, which is why it is called the great bliss chakra. In the throat is *the complete gathering of enjoyment chakra,* which has sixteen spokes, and opens upward. It is through the mouth that we experience all that we eat and drink, which is why it is called the complete gathering of enjoyment chakra. Everything that enters the body goes through the throat. At the heart is *the dharma chakra* that has eight spokes and faces downwards. All thoughts of the three times are formed by the mind, which is why it is called the dharma chakra. At the navel is *the emanation chakra,* which has forty-two spokes and faces upwards. The chakra at the heart faces down and the one at the navel faces up. It is from the navel that in the beginning the whole body is formed. All those chakras are formed by those spokes, which are hollow inside like soda straws. When teaching tsa lung practice, it is good to have the drawings. Karmey Khenpo drew many of these.

Think well about the teachings you have received on the vase and secret empowerments. If you are unable to visualize a deity with pure recollection, vivid presence, and stable pride, then it is difficult to proceed on this path, as in the secret empowerment you need to visualize as well. You actually have to train; merely reading about the teachings does not have any benefit. Anything that you become familiar with becomes easy to apply. I have to teach the monks in

---

1 The one at the secret place is called *the sustaining bliss chakra* that has sixty-four spokes and faces downwards.

the three-year retreat center at my monastery in Bir, India. When I first go in and talk about *powa* and the six doctrines of Naropa, they are convinced that they cannot do it. So, for a couple of days, I have them check it out. After one week or eight days, all of them have some signs of powa practice—blood or pus from the aperture of Brahma—a symbol that they have trained properly. This has been the case with many monks. Also, the fire of *tummo* has blazed forth for many of them. That is because they have become familiar with the practice. Just listening to teachings, as you all like to do, has no benefit. You will merely grow old.

THE ROOT TEXT

THE SECRET EMPOWERMENT
Lamrim Yeshe Nyingpo

The Wisdom Essence of Oral Instructions in the
Stages of the Path

The Heart Essence of Padmasambhava according to
The Guru's Heart Practice of Dorje Drakpo Tsal,
Powerful Vajra Wrath

Spoken by Padmasambhava
Recorded by Khandro Yeshe Tsogyal
Revealed and decoded by Chokgyur Lingpa *and*
Jamyang Khyentse Wangpo

In particular, the way of corrective subjugation ཿ
Is to protect yourself and repel adversity ཿ
With the key points of fortress, passage, life-force, and fruition; ཿ
To separate the joined with the ritual of slaying, ཿ
And at the end to conclude the activity by suppressing, throwing off,
     and burning. ཿ

For the supreme activity, the unexcelled and highest, ཿ
The bam sadhana that pacifies violations and breaches, ཿ

Carefully examine for qualifications, the auspicious and pure bam. ཿ
Acquire it with yogic discipline and vajra gait. ཿ
Place it in the center of the mandala, visualize it as the deity,
     Approach, and Accomplishment. ཿ
When the signs such as lights, sounds, and fragrance occur, ཿ
The deity melts into light, in the manner of dissolving deity into
     deity. ཿ
Enjoy the great vajra bliss of indivisible subject and object, ཿ
And promote delight to mend breaches. ཿ

Having in this way taken as basis the accomplishments of
     Mahayoga ཿ
Which are chiefly the practices of the vase empowerment, ཿ
Now, for the Full Approach, the gradual path of the secret
     empowerment, ཿ
The Anu Yoga path, the support and the supported, ཿ
The profound development stage of channels, energies, and bindu
     essences, ཿ
Meaning that the self-occurred world and its inhabitants, from the
     moment they were formed, ཿ
Are, themselves, an uncontrived mandala. ཿ

Within the bhaga of the consort, the concepts of the four elements ཿ
Are the great celestial palace of the gross aggregates ཿ

3

Where the five sense doors, flesh, blood, warmth, breath, and so
    forth
Shine as the majestic splendor of ornaments and decorations.
Roma is the daka and *kyangma* is the dakini.
The central is *Shri Heruka*, Samantabhadra.

All the wheel centers are the peaceful and wrathful chiefs of the
    supreme families.
All the channel spokes are the lords and ladies of these families.
The body is the samaya and bindu, the samadhi sattva.
Through the pride of undivided awareness wisdom,
Take delight in sense pleasures and enjoyments as the cloud of great
    bliss.
Extolling the superior virtues is songs of praise.
Movements are mudras; walking and sitting are vajra dances.
Inhaling and exhaling breath are unceasing recitation.
Food and drink are the constantly enjoyed torma and ganachakra.

The luminous deity satisfied by the bliss of union
Is manifest from the bindu and vanishes into emptiness in the
    nada.
From the state of emptiness, all sights, sounds, and thoughts
Are spontaneously present inseparably from the supreme three
    vajras.

Whoever becomes adept in this profound development stage,
With pliant mind-energy, will accomplish the eyes and higher
    perceptions.

Heat and signs will arise effortlessly,
Thus the body of great bliss becomes the support.
Now for the supported, the completion stage of channel, energies,
    and essences:
With the right body posture, train in (focusing upon the) inhalation
    and exhalation of breath.

The essence is bliss-emptiness; the form is the yidam deity.§
The expressions are the crisp display of the reflection of the moon in
    water.§
In the center of this rainbow-like body is the *dhuti* channel.§
Lalana and *pingala* are to the right and left.§
Amidst these three are based:§
The "fully arrayed summit" with thirty-two petals,§
The "taste gatherer" with eight doubling into sixteen,§
The "fully placed recollector," with the petals of the eight
    gatherings,§
And the "creating wheel" with sixty-four.§

When having become practiced in visualizing these according to
    their structure,§
Completely expel the defective energies.§
Fully lead the flawless in the upper, lower, and middle parts.§
Fill like a vase, distribute, and shoot out like an arrow.§
Develop effort gradually, by being uninterrupted.§

Your body will be blissful, your speech melodious, your mind still,
    and you will accomplish immortality.§
In the session breaks do yogic exercises and rest peacefully.§
At times, practice stillness of mind through vajra-recitation.§

Having become practiced in that, beneath the nirmana wheel§
Is the concealed natural form of knowledge, *Chandali.*§
Visualize the A stroke and kindle it, inciting it with the energies.§
Entering the central pathway, invoke the deities of the wheels.§

The blissful essence from the HANG at the crown of the head§
Reinvigorates it, and again it blazes more and more.§
By the channels and elements being filled with heat and bliss,§
Actualize nonconceptual wisdom and bring it to the space of
    dharmata.§

The Approach and Full Approach of this profound development
    stage§
Are the energy practices together with the yogic exercises.§
By the Accomplishment of *Chandali* you will realize§
The Great Accomplishment of undivided bliss and emptiness.§

Regard all daytime post-meditations as subsidiaries of this path,§
Impurely, as the eight analogies of illusion,§
And purely, as only mind, the apparent-empty form of the deity.§
Delight in the magical bliss of the path of learning by emerging§
In the mudra of mind-energy, and of the union of the path of no
    learning.§

Having realized the nature of all phenomena to be emptiness and
    luminosity,§
At the time of sleep, meditate evenly on the indestructible bindu at
    the center of the heart.§
By leading through the experiences of the four stages of emptiness,§
The example and meaning luminosities will effortlessly dawn.§

In the post-meditation, through the force of aspiration and energy
    practice,§
Recognize dreams and train in the great skill of transforming
    apparitions.§
Dissolve into the state of great emptiness, and as the illusory
    manifestation of compassion,§
Accomplish the single and elaborate mudras and the group
    assemblies filling the space.§

If you have not perfected the training within this lifetime,§
Gather mind-energy, eject, and rest in that state.§
Join together by mixing the sights, sounds, and thoughts of the
    bardo§
With deity, mantra, and the great wisdom.§

In this way, channels and essences are the deities of undivided
    samaya and wisdom.⸪
Through the threefold self-existence, visualization, and training,⸪
Take the wisdoms of enlightened body, speech, and mind as the
    path.⸪
Prana-union is empowerment and vajra recitation.⸪
Make offerings with the *chandali* fire and praises with the song of
    the blazing and dripping.⸪
Within the pleasant assembly hall permeated by warmth,⸪
Delight in the feast and torma of the enjoyments of melting bliss.⸪
Dissolve in the state of nonthought and emerge as the illusory form
    of the deity.⸪
Reverse order is the space of luminous suchness.⸪
Progressive order is the all-illuminating and the cloud of the seed
    syllable.⸪

By training in the skill of the single and elaborate forms in dreams,⸪
And through the group-gathering practice of undivided mind-
    energy,⸪
As the maturation, the three doors will be transformed into the
    three vajras,⸪
And the supreme siddhi of the three kayas spontaneously present as
    birth, death, and bardo,⸪
Will be naturally manifest without effort.⸪

When your experience and realization in any of these have greatly
    increased,⸪
Then, for the practice of the wisdom-knowledge empowerment,⸪
· ·

Through the mudra, sign deity of Great Attainment of Prophecy,⸪
You reach to the end of the Perfection of the Great Strength of
    abandonment and attainment,⸪
And your experience becomes of one taste with that of the Heruka.⸪

THE COMMENTARY

PART 3

The Light of Wisdom, Vol. III

THE SECRET EMPOWERMENT

by Jamgön Kongtrül

A Commentary on the Wisdom Essence of
Oral Instructions in the Stages of the Path,
According to Lamey Tukdrub Dorje Draktsal,
The Guru's Heart Practice of Powerful Vajra Wrath,
Entitled Fully Spreading the Light of Wisdom

ACTIVITIES

24

The All-Encompassing Activities

The Means for Accomplishing the All-Encompassing Activities Based on the Root Mandala

This section has two parts: A general explanation of the person who can accomplish the activities and a detailed explanation specifying the activities to be accomplished.

GENERAL EXPLANATION OF THE PERSON WHO CAN ACCOMPLISH THE ACTIVITIES

The *Lamrim Yeshe Nyingpo* root text says:

> Moreover, the yogi who has attained the heat of the path,⁸

DETAILED EXPLANATION SPECIFYING THE ACTIVITIES TO BE ACCOMPLISHED

This has seven topics: Consecration, fire offering, elixir extraction (*rasayana*), guiding the departed, activities of acceptance and subjugation, *bam*, and *amrita sadhana*.

Consecration
Fire Offering
Concluding Activities

Subjugating

The *Lamrim Yeshe Nyingpo* root text says:

In particular, the way of corrective subjugation⁸
Is to protect yourself, and repel adversity⁸
With the key points of fortress, passage, life-force, and
fruition;⁸
To separate the joined with the ritual of slaying,⁸
And at the end to conclude the activity by suppressing,
throwing off and burning.⁸

Bam Sadhana

The sixth topic, the supreme sadhana of the great bam has two
points: a brief statement and a detailed explanation.

Brief Statement

The *Lamrim Yeshe Nyingpo* root text says:

For the supreme activity, the unexcelled and highest,⁸
The bam sadhana that pacifies violations and breaches,⁸

Detailed Explanation

The *Lamrim Yeshe Nyingpo* root text says:

Carefully examine for qualifications, the auspicious and
pure bam.⁸
Acquire it with yogic discipline and vajra gait.⁸

Place it in the center of the mandala, visualize it as the
  deity, Approach, and Accomplishment.[note]
When the signs such as lights, sounds, and fragrance
  occur,[note]
The deity melts into light, in the manner of dissolving deity
  into deity.[note]
Enjoy the great vajra bliss of indivisible subject and object,[note]
And promote delight to mend breaches.[note]

Amrita Sadhana

25

The Path of Accomplishing

Detailed Explanation of the Practice of Group Assembly

26

The Result

Explaining the Time of Achieving the Four Vidyadhara Levels as the Result of Practice

The Practice of the Secret Empowerment

The practices connected to the secret empowerment, the stages for conferring blessings upon oneself, have two aspects: a brief presentation, connecting with the above, and a detailed explanation of that.

BRIEF STATEMENT CONNECTING WITH THE ABOVE

The *Lamrim Yeshe Nyingpo* root text says:

> Having in this way taken as basis the accomplishments of
> Mahayoga
> Which are chiefly the practices of the vase empowerment,
> Now, for the Full Approach, the gradual path of the secret
> empowerment,

In this way, one has taken as basis the development stage, together with its subsidiary aspects, which is the main method for practicing the vase empowerment, the root of the four empowerments. Accomplishing the Approach related to the tantras of Mahayoga, or "great yoga," is the stepping-stone for the higher paths. Now we come to the Full Approach stage of the path in which the practitioner takes as the path the profound wisdom that is obtained through the secret empowerment into the mandala of the body and practices the wisdom-knowledge empowerment.

DETAILED EXPLANATION

The detailed explanation has two parts: the actual path and the inclusion of other aspects of the path together with the results.

The Actual Path

This has two aspects: a brief statement and a detailed explanation.

Brief Satement

The *Lamrim Yeshe Nyingpo* root text says:

> The Anu Yoga path, the support and the supported,
> The profound development stage of channels, energies, and
>   bindu essences,
> Meaning that the self-occurred world and its inhabitants,
>   from the moment they were formed,
> Are, themselves, an uncontrived mandala.

This path connected with the statements of the completion *Anu Yoga*, which means "subsequent yoga," entails binding the key points of the *vajra* body—the support—together with channel, energy, and essence that it supports. Being more profound than the preceding stage, it is known as the profound development stage. It means that from the moment when the elements of channels, energies, and essences are initially formed, they are spontaneously a mandala comprised of the natural world—the "circle"—and its inhabitants—the center.[2] This is called "the spontaneously present mandala of the body"; it is not a fabrication of something that did not exist and that we would be superimposing mentally. So, it is vastly superior, just as the *Magical Key to the Treasury* mentions:[3]

> The completion Anu Yoga
> Is to accept that aggregates, elements, and sense sources

Are the mandala of male and female deities
In the manner of uncreated perfection.

Drilbupa has also stated:

All these beings by nature are
Indivisible from the perfect mandala.

In general, it is crucial to understand the nature of the vajra body
in order to apply the key points related to it. The reason is that the
subtle aspects of body, speech, and mind are from the very beginning utterly pure as the deity of the threefold indestructible vajra.
These three, moreover, are in their ultimate identity the six families
of deities and consorts—the pure essence of the five elements with
the pure aspect of mind as the sixth. By combining these in sets of
two, the pure essences of earth and water are the vajra body, the pure
essences of fire and wind are the vajra speech, and the pure essences
of space and mind form the vajra mind. This triple division is merely
in terms of aspects, while ultimately there is the great equality of the
vajra body, speech, and mind. This is the "basis for purification."[4]

Their natural radiance from the perspective of relative perception is the right, left, and central channels, which serve as the support
for semen, uterine blood, and the energies, and, since the mind-energy has a joint function, it is also the support for mind. When the
coarse aspects are formed, the features of body appear from the
channels, those of voice from the energies, and those of mind from
the essences. These three doors of delusion are the "objects of to be
purified."[5]

The "purifying means" are the extraordinary profound paths
related to the three higher empowerments, which bind their functioning and purify them into luminosity. In so doing, when all temporary obscurations have dissolved into primordial wisdom, one
accomplishes the "result of purification," the unobscured three *kayas*
permeated by great bliss.

There are four points briefly to describe this principle: the causes and conditions that form the body, the structuring channels, the moving energies, and the placement of the essences.

The Causes and Conditions that Form the Body

For the first, the human body on the Jambu continent, endowed with the six elements, is the extraordinary support for Vajrayana practice. It is produced through a combination of three factors: the obscured mind as the forming factor, the closure of karmic actions as the cause, and the meeting of a father and mother as the circumstance. This combination—phrased as sun, moon, and Rahula—refers to the father's sperm, the mother's blood, and the *bardo* consciousness, and it is from these three that body, voice, and mind are produced.

The bardo consciousness forms the five elements in the following way. The earth element is formed by experiencing solidity in the contract between the father and mother, water from the liquid nature of the *bodhichitta* fluid, fire from the heat that arises from their stirring, wind from the bodhichitta moving through the channels, and the element of space from the bliss. The body is formed when they come together with the sixth element of consciousness, which is wakefulness. While remaining in the mother's womb for the duration of the ten months that correspond to the nature of the ten *bhumis,* the first channels to be formed are the three primary ones followed by the 54,000 [others]. The phase of forming the body is completed when the 72,000 channels are formed on the third month after birth.

The Structuring Channels

Stretching from the secret place to the *ushnisha,* the *avadhuti* channel is in the middle of the body, similar to a life pillar, and connects to the spot between the eyebrows at its upper end. To its right side is the *roma* and to the left the *kyangma.*[6] These two connect to the nostrils at their upper ends, and all three channels are parallel from the level of the eyebrows. On the way down, the three channels interconnect in a "knot" at the center point of each of the four chakras, and they join below the navel at the lower end of the central channel.[7] Then, the lower extremity of the central channel called "the conch-shaped" goes to the right and expels or withholds sperm, the kyangma goes to middle and expels or withholds urine, while the roma goes to left and expels or withholds blood and feces.

In the centers of each of the four chakras—at the crown, throat, heart, and navel—four channels branch out into the four directions. At the heart level, these four branch into two each, making eight. At the throat, they branch into a further two each, making sixteen. At the crown, they again split into a further two, making thirty-two. At the navel, four of the eight that branched out at the heart, split into two each, thereby making the twelve channels of transition.[8] There are sixty-four in all when the eight channels that have branched divide into five each, while the four that did not branch each divide into six.[9]

Moreover, at the crown is the body chakra or "wheel of great bliss," so called because it is where dwells the syllable HANG, which is the support of great bliss. At the throat is the speech chakra and also the site for tasting the six kinds of taste, so it is known as the "wheel of enjoyment." The channel petals at the heart center are called the mind chakra or the "wheel of Dharma." The navel is known as the "wheel of emanation" since it is the first part of the body to be formed and also because it is the site of emanation, or the location from whence emanations permeate the three realms.[10] All these are called wheels because their spokes and so forth have a similar shape and because they behave like wheels in interrupting conceptual thinking by binding their respective functions.

When all these channels divide further, there are also those of the inner twenty-four places and thirty-seven lands, as well as the 24,000 channels, which, when associated with the three main channels—roma, kyangma, and avadhuti—add up to 72,000.[11] These branch further into an uncountable number, corresponding to the number of pores on the body.

It is furthermore taught that the number of chakras cannot be categorically decided, since the ushnisha at the upper end of the central channel, the secret chakra at its lower end, and so forth, can be added. In short, the yogi should be aware there are the 72,000 channels, the channels that form the wheels that are the primary among them, and the thirty-two channels, which among these are the most important, and so on.

It is also mentioned that the six chakras retain the pure essences related to the mind-energy and that their impure parts generate disease. That is to say, disease due to phlegm is generated by the ushnisha and the forehead chakras, disease due to bile from the throat and heart, wind disorders from the outer circuit of the navel and secret place, and combination diseases from the inner circuit of the secret place.

Furthermore, the body has three aspects—coarse, subtle, and extremely subtle—and the nature of all three is the "ultimate wisdom channel." Since this channel appears in the form of self-knowing, it is present as the "pervader" of all ordinary channels and, therefore, is also known as the "great central channel of original wakefulness." As it is all-encompassing, all relative channels proceed from it and, therefore, the ordinary channels function in a way that corresponds to how the yogi directs his or her attention. This is why one should understand the key point that though various tantras present the channels in different ways, these teachings are not in opposition with one another.

The Moving Energies

Third, generally speaking, the attributes of voice of all embodied creatures, as well as the characteristic of time, like exhalation spans, hours, or days, have as their basis for arising the ultimate wisdom energy, otherwise known as the energy of the great life force.[12] The *Magical Net of Manjushri* describes this:

> The great life force, without arising,
> Beyond verbal utterance,
> Is the supreme cause of all uttering,
> Which fully clarifies every word.

In accordance with this statement, it is the basic nature of every kind of energy and forms the basis for the "causal tantra" that permeates incessantly.[13] Its temporary defilement, which has the nature of the all-ground consciousness, is the movement of mind towards objects and is known as the wind of karma. This karmic wind, which serves as the support for the five aggregates, has five primary energies—the life-upholding, the upward-moving, the pervading, the fire-accompanying, and the downward-clearing—that are also known as the primary aggregate-energies. Their functions are, respectively, to support the life force; maintain respiration; maintain the body; ensure its temperature; and perform the functions of walking, sitting, and excreting or holding feces, urine, and sperm. If it happens that these energies reverse, they can create the diseases of, respectively, fainting, insanity, death, and the like; illness in the upper torso; paralysis; abdominal disorders; and sickness in the lower torso. It is also explained that these energies are situated, respectively, in the center of the body, in the upper part, out to the extremities of the skin, in the area of digestion, and from the navel downward.

The five subsidiary energies—known as circulating, fully circulating, truly circulating, completely circulating, and definitely circulating—are situated in the five sense faculties, where they perform their different functions and so forth. In particular, the energies circulating to the nose move, during one full day and night, in the number of 21,600 times. Moreover, in terms of the twelve transitions, from the sixty-four channel petals of the navel, the four branches that previously split into six are the transitions of the central channel. Therefore, since they do not descend into the mandala,[14] they are known as the four empty channels.[15] Circulating through the remaining sixty channels, the subsidiary energies intermingle with the energies of the navel and all the energies of the channel wheels along the channel path all the way to the little hairs of the body. Thus, they reach to the opening of the nostrils through the pathways of the roma and kyangma.

Furthermore, due to the sequence of retraction and expansion, left and right of the five elements, each transition consists of five half hours [dbyug gu].[16] Each half-hour period consists of 360 breaths, so that during each transition, there are eighteen hundred movements of breath. In addition, due to the division of the four empty channels, one part out of each thirty-two divisions of one breath is a wisdom energy.[17] When these are accumulated, each half hour has 11¼ breaths of wisdom energy, and during each transition there are fixed on a part of 256 fractions. During a full day and night they move 675 times. When phrasing that in terms of a period [chu tshod], one period has one time division [chu srang] and three breaths.[18] When these are counted, during one month there are fifty-six such powers and fifteen [chu chung]. By these being repeated twelve times, they make eleven days and fifteen hours, which is the amount of wisdom energies during one year. This is also a cause for the external month delay. When the wisdom energies of a hundred-year-old person are added together, they amount to three years and three fortnights.[19] These and other such details are taught extensively in the tantras.

The colors of the energies of earth, water, fire, wind, and space are, respectively, yellow, white, red, black, and blue. Their extent is that they go from four fingers below the navel up to the tip of the nose and between twelve and sixteen fingers into the distance.[20]

Among all these energies, the ones that move through the nostrils and perform movement, and so forth, are called coarse. The ones that do not move inside the body, the energies of the five elements that have a samsaric nature, the ten energies of expression, and all the carriages that move the myriad thoughts are middling. All the energies that are the carriages of the four levels of experience are subtle, while the energies that are carriages for the special luminosity are extremely subtle. Corresponding to the various pith instructions, there are a variety of different presentations of energies. However, since the wisdom energy is all-encompassing, and since these other energies are all its followers, they are included within this single key point. This is why it is taught that the coarse karmic energy becomes wisdom energy and produces its qualities when bound.[21, 22]

The Placement of the Essences

There are two aspects to the fourth topic—the *bindu* of wisdom and the bindu of consciousness. The first of these is the root of all bindus, which serves as the support for the causal tantra. It is taught using the names "bindu of the wisdom essence" or "the indestructible bindu," and it remains as the identity of unconfined empty cognizance.

The second bindu is described as three: the bindus of energy, mantra, and substance. The energy-bindu is due to the force of the indestructible bindu at the heart center, the self-liberation of dualistic experience by means of binding the energies.[23] The mantra bindu is so called because visualizing the bindu marked with the deity at the tip of the nose[24] protects the mind from clinging to ordinary experience. The substance bindu is, for instance, the experience of bliss, which arises from visualizing the bindu below the tip of nose.[25]

To explain the last of these a little further, there are two aspects—the pure and the impure[26]—related to the two elements, the white and the red. The white element situated at the crown of the head is received from the father and has the nature of HANG, and the red element at the confluence of the three channels below the navel is received from the mother and has the nature of the A-*tung*; these are the rulers of all the body's white and red elements. They are supported by the proximity of the central channel, and they serve as the support for consciousness.

From them appear the two aspects: the pure and the impure. Generated in connection with the mother's channel in the womb, after taking birth they, [the pure and the impure] treat all the food and drink in the belly, break up putrefaction with phlegm, transform its color with bile, and by means of the heat of the energy's equalizing fire, they digest and process decay. For this the pure parts become blood in the liver, and passing through the veins turn into flesh, and successively into fat, bone, marrow, and bodhichitta through which it becomes strength and radiance. The impure parts of all these, successively are feces, bile, skin, glands, teeth, and nails, internal impurities, spittle, mucus, and so forth. Because of spilling out at the end of pleasure, it is known as seven body components.

Regarding their distinctive types, there are twenty-four essential elements, from the indivisible at the crown of the head down to the production of teeth and nails. Each of these is again divided into three—dissolution, enjoyment, and owner—which makes seventy-two essential elements. When further divided into a thousand each, there are 72,000 essential elements, which can yet again be divided into a thousand each to make 72 million. In this way it is taught that every single channel is permeated by energy and every single energy is permeated by bindu.[27]

The yoga tantras teach that in addition to the twenty-four elements, there are thirty-two when adding five including the three primary channels, the triple combined and so forth. The *Heruka Galpo* mentions:

> In the body there are thirty-two
> Channels through which the bodhichitta moves.

In addition, it also seems there is the explanation that when adding the bindus that move through the five primary energies, not including the great life force, there are thirty-six.[28]

It is also explained that all of these bindus transit in relationship with the wisdom bindu due to the coursing of all the four joys within the four chakras. And it is also explained that these bindus are known as the transitional life-retainers in combination with the consciousness that is the identity of the strength or power or vital force in the body.

To summarize, all the bindus can be included within three substances—semen, blood, and *tamas*—and these three produce desire, anger, and delusion. From them arise the eighty innate thought states and by them karma is formed, which gives rise to the myriad types of misery of deluded experiences.

When binding these three to be unchanging, one reverses from samsara and—since the root of all the bindus is the indestructible bindu of *dharmata* which is all-encompassing—one should understand the key point that every possible type of yoga involving the examined or unexamined bindus will either directly or indirectly become the true path.[29][30]

These points are presented as they are widely known in the general sections of tantra, while the extraordinary and specific system of the Luminous Great Perfection is, as you find it, extensively explained in the *Precious Treasury of the Supreme Vehicle* and other sources.

Detailed Explanation

This has two aspects: explaining how to visualize the vajra body that is the support and the explanation of the yogas of the channels, energies, and essences that are supported.

Explaining How to Visualize the Vajra Body that Is the Support

The first of these also has two aspects: the actual path and the result of training in it.

The Actual Path

For the first, the *Lamrim Yeshe Nyingpo* root text says:

Within the bhaga of the consort, the concepts of the four
　　elements,ᵉ
Are the great celestial palace of the gross aggregatesᵉ
Where the five sense doors, flesh, blood, warmth, breath,
　　and so forthᵉ
Shine as the majestic splendor of ornaments and
　　decorations.ᵉ
Roma is the daka and *kyangma* is the dakini.ᵉ
The central is *Shri Heruka,* Samantabhadra.ᵉ

All the wheel centers are the peaceful and wrathful chiefs of
　　the supreme families.ᵉ
All the channel spokes are the lords and ladies of these
　　families.ᵉ
The body is the samaya and bindu, the samadhi sattva.ᵉ
Through the pride of undivided awareness wisdom,ᵉ
Take delight in sense pleasures and enjoyments as the cloud
　　of great bliss.ᵉ
Extolling the superior virtues are songs of praise.ᵉ
Movements are mudras; walking and sitting are vajra
　　dances.ᵉ
Inhaling and exhaling breath are unceasing recitation.ᵉ
Food and drink are the constantly enjoyed torma and
　　ganachakra.ᵉ

The luminous deity satisfied by the bliss of unionᵉ
Is manifest from the bindu and vanishes into emptiness in
　　the *nada.*ᵉ
From the state of emptiness, all sights, sounds, and
　　thoughtsᵉ
Are spontaneously present inseparably from the supreme
　　three vajras.ᵉ

How is this profound development stage the uncontrived and
self-existing mandala? The gradually layered four elements, together

with the source-of-dharmas, are naturally present as the gathering of the four elements in the womb due to the circumstance of the initial joining of the father and mother. Among these, the E—that is the mother's *bhaga*—is the support for appropriating it by means of the mind-energy's conception. It is here that the vast celestial palace is formed as the coarse aggregate of physical form.

In more detail, the body, which measures two arms in length, is the square celestial palace. Its eight subsidiary parts are the eight pillars. The five sense organs, the faculties through which the five elemental energies move, give rise to the eyes, which are the windows of the sun and moon, as well as the four doors, which are the ears, nose, mouth, and the lower opening. The flesh is the basis of the mandala. The blood is the lakes and ponds, its warmth is the master flames, the breath is the rainbow light, and so forth. This includes the heart, which is the jewel ornament on the peak of all the *chitta*-crests; the entrails that are the pendants; the fingers that are the crescents and mirrors; the teeth which are the railings; the tongue, which is the upper storey; the eight openings that are the charnel grounds; the hair, skin, and bone joints, which are the protection circle, and so on. In this way the supports are the spontaneously perfected celestial palace, consisting of these self-existing adornments and decorations, blazing in majestic splendor. Inside, the roma on the right is the *dakas*, the means, while the kyangma to the left is the *dakinis*, the knowledge. The central channel is the great *heruka* of universal splendor, the all-pervasive sovereign Samantabhadra. The five chakra locations are, respectively, the peaceful or wrathful central figures belonging to the five supreme families—the Buddha family at the crown, Padma at the throat, Vajra at the heart center, Ratna at the navel, and Karma at the secret center. These central figures are either Vairochana or Buddha Heruka, and so forth. Together with the channel petals on these chakras, which are the male and female mandala clusters of the minor families, these are spontaneously perfected as mandala deities, which are the supported.[31]

Moreover, the outer physical body is the *samaya* being while the inner pure bindu is the *samadhi* being. The awareness that pervades them is the wisdom being. In this way these three are from the beginning formed in the way that is indivisible. With the pride of knowing this to be as it is, the completing subsidiary aspects are to recognize as follows:

That all kinds of sense pleasures, no matter how they may appear, are, as objects of the five senses, the cloud banks of offerings of great bliss, and to enjoy them free from accepting or rejecting. That all eulogy by others proclaiming the superior virtues are songs of praise. That all movements are mudras. That walking and sitting are vajra dances. That the three aspects of exhalation, inhalation, and retaining the energies comprised of life and force are naturally perfected as vajra recitation so that it is uninterrupted always throughout day and night. That all types of food and drink are enjoyed always as the inner *torma* and *ganachakra*. That the wisdom deity of luminosity, which is pleased through the bliss of the four joys in the four centers during the time of union, gradually manifests from the sixteen aspects of the bindus, [32] when the coemergent and indestructible *nada* dissolves at the final moment of the four levels of emptiness[33]. The practice of the development stage, with a mental image, along with its branches, enters into the inconceivable completion stage.

That, from the state of emptiness, every visible form, audible sound, and the host of thought movements are spontaneously perfected as being indivisible from the supreme state of the threefold vajra body, vajra speech, and vajra mind.

The meaning of *nada* in this context is the identity of the extremely subtle threefold principle of energy and elements, which is indestructible until the end of the stream. It symbolizes the extremely subtle attributes with form.[34]

This type of development stage is described in the *Assemblage of Knowledge Scripture* by the following words:

The outer, inner, and secret mandalas,⚶
Displayed within the primordially all-encompassing great
    perfection of Samantabhadra,⚶
Are pure appearance and existence, the realm of male and
    female deities.⚶

The Result of Training in the Path

The *Lamrim Yeshe Nyingpo* root text says:

Whoever becomes adept in this profound development
    stage,⚶
With pliant mind-energy, will accomplish the eyes and
    higher perceptions.⚶
Heat and signs will arise effortlessly,⚶

Any yogi who grows accustomed to and familiar with the profound development stage, which has been described here in such a way, will before long, by practicing, give rise to an extraordinary state of samadhi due to the pliancy of his or her mind-energy, and he or she will also attain the five eyes and the superknowledges. The five eyes are the flesh eye that sees material things up to the distance of a hundred or thousand furlongs; the *deva* eye that sees all sentient beings die, transmigrate, and take rebirth; the knowledge eye that sees the nature of dharmata exactly as it is; the dharma eye that perceives the minds of others to a level that equals one's personal abandonment and realization; and the buddha eye that sees the true enlightenment of all phenomena. The first two are caused by karmic ripening, while all of them are caused by the power of practice.

The six superknowledges are the purity of body, which is miraculous powers; the purity of speech, which is divine hearing; the perception of other's minds; the purity of mind, which is the recognition of former lives; divine sight; and the superknowledge of the extinction of defilements. It is taught regarding the five eyes and six superknowledges that the five eyes can be possessed by ordinary beings, as well as all noble beings on the bhumis. On the other hand, each of the superknowledges is comprised of the state of buddhahood, and even noble beings possess only their resemblance.

Furthermore, the yogi will effortlessly and spontaneously experience the amazing types of outer, inner, and innermost signs of heat, as well as signs and indications in actuality, meditative vision, or in dreams. One tantra describes this in the following words:

> The outer, the inner, and the suchness,
> The concrete and the inconcrete, and the natural state
> Are all the mandala of the vajra body,
> And the all-ground wisdom is the self-existing deity.
> Whoever trains and grows familiar to become stable
> Will, before a long time has passed
> Experience that every perception, whether asleep or awake,
> It is the totality of the outer and inner buddha field.

Explanation of the Supported, the Yogas of the Channels, Energies, and Essences

Second, the explanation of the yogas of channels, energies, and essences has three parts: connecting with a brief statement and a detailed explanation of its meaning.

Connecting With a Brief Statement

For the first, the *Lamrim Yeshe Nyingpo* root text says:

> Thus, the body of great bliss becomes the support.§
> Now for the supported, the completion stage of channels,
>   energies, and essences:§

After having taken as support the bodily form of this self-existing vajra body of great bliss, by means of the supported—the yogas of channels, energies and essences—the following describes the completion stage of self-consecration.

Detailed Explanation of the Topic

The detailed explanation of its meaning has three aspects: training the structuring channels, training the moving energies, and training the essence-bodhichitta.[35]

Training the Structured Channels

For the first, the *Lamrim Yeshe Nyingpo* root text says:

> With the right body posture, train in (focusing upon the)
>   inhalation and exhalation of breath.
> The essence is bliss-emptiness; the form is the yidam deity.
> The expressions are the crisp display of the reflection of the
>   moon in water.
> In the center of this rainbow-like body is the *dhuti*
>   channel.
> *Lalana* and *pingala* are to the right and left; amidst these
>   three are based:
> The "fully arrayed summit" with thirty-two petals,
> The "taste gatherer" with eight doubling into sixteen,
> The "fully placed recollector," with the petals of the eight
>   gatherings,
> And the "creating wheel" with sixty-four.
> When having become practiced in visualizing these
>   according to their structure,

To explain this, the body resembles a city, the energies resemble a blind horse, while consciousness resembles a crippled man trying to steer it. Unless he controls its movements, the horse upon which he rides will go astray in the streets. Likewise, if he does manage to control it by blocking the exit, the man and the horse will join so that they cannot move. Therefore, it is of utmost importance to control the key points of the body for binding the energies that are the carriers of conceptual thinking. The *Longchen Rabjam* tantra explains this:[36]

> Place your legs in the vajra posture.
> Cross your two hands in equanimity.
> Straighten your body like that of an arrow.
> Expand your shoulders like a vulture's wings,
> Then your neck like a mighty arrow.
> Raise your bodily parts like the crest of a boar.
> Keep in tune, one-pointedly, your eyes, the tip of your nose,
>   and mind.[37]

Accordingly, while your body maintains these key points, rein in while focusing on each of them. In order to expel the poisons of the *klesha* energies contained inside, expel the stale breath three times through your nostrils. The key point of mind is to imagine that the perception of your ordinary body vanishes into basic space and that from within this state of nonthought you imagine that your bodily form appears like that of a rainbow in the sky—in identity it is of a blissful and empty nature, while in appearance it is the bodily form of the *yidam* deity and in expression it is vivid and clear, without haziness, and unobstructed, like the manifestation of the moon in water.

In the center of your body, which is visualized in this form, is the channel that is famous under the name "avadhuti." It is blue and like a pillar. It is present from the opening of Brahma to the secret place and is endowed with four characteristics.[38] On its right and left sides are the red roma and the white kyangma, which flank the *dhuti* such that the three of them are parallel. The upper ends of the roma and kyangma bend forward at the top of the head and connect with the two nostrils. The two lower ends connect with the dhuti at the level of four fingers below the navel. While these three principle channels are upright like a life pillar, they support the chakras like the spokes of an umbrella in the following way.

The wheel of the completely arrayed summit [39] at the crown of the head has thirty-two spokes.[40] The wheel of the complete gathering of taste at the throat has two sets of eight spokes, making sixteen. The wheel of the total placement of recollection at the heart center has eight spokes that support the eight collections. The wheel of the generation at the navel has sixty-four spokes.[41]

From the center of each of these four wheels, channel petals branch out from the dhuti into the four directions, and each of these bears the properties of the four elements. At the heart center, each of these four branch into a further two to make an outer circle of eight. At the throat, each of these is yet further divided into two to make an intermediate circle of eight and an outer circle of sixteen. At the crown, these again divide into two each, so that the secondary intermediate circle has sixteen while there are thirty-two in the outer circle. At the navel, four of the eight branching out, like at the heart center, divide into two and these secondary eight divide into five each, while each of the original four that do not divide into two split into six such that the intermediate circle has twelve and the outer circle has sixty-four.[42]

You should bring to mind exactly how these are present in the body. Visualize all these channels in a form that is vivid, clear, and hollow. Since these hollow channels serve as the basis for everything, when you have grown thoroughly familiar with them, you should embark on the following yoga.

Training the Moving Energies

The second has two parts: the practice during the session and the practice during the breaks.

The Practice During the Session

The first of these also has two aspects: the principle vase-shaped practice and the result of this training.

The Principle Vase-Shaped Practice

The *Lamrim Yeshe Nyingpo* root text says:

> Completely expel the defective energies.᠎
> Fully lead the flawless in the upper, lower, and middle
>   parts.᠎
> Fill like a vase, distribute, and shoot out like an arrow.᠎
> Develop effort gradually, by being uninterrupted.᠎

After visualizing the hollowness of the channels, the key point of body, you, completely expel through the nostrils the energies that, prior to this, have remained inside, mingled with the imperfections of the three poisons. This expulsion should be done nine or three times.

With skill in the key point concerning the timing of the energies, including the wisdom energy that circulates evenly, you should inhale through the nostrils the energies that are the pure parts of the five elements and free of shortcomings, retracting the upper energy and the downward-clearing energy, so that the two lower energies, completely brought up to the navel center, flow together and unite in the central channel, filling it like a vase. Without suppressing, pull and press from the right and left as well as distributing outside and inside. Once you cannot hold the breath any longer, let it shoot out like an arrow.[43] Gradually increase the force of effort in the prana practice that is endowed with these four applications.[44] By continuing the training daily without break, even though your body or mind may feel tired, you will accomplish the authentic measure of the vase-shaped practice in either the foremost, middling, or lesser degree, as it has been explained in the *Samvarodaya Tantra*. Nevertheless, for your present practice, use the time it takes to make one round with the palm of your hand touching each kneecap and snapping your fingers once as the measure. In this way, thirty-six measures equals the lesser vase-shaped practice, seventy-two the middling, and 108 is regarded as the measure for the big blocking.[45]

The Result of the Training

The *Lamrim Yeshe Nyingpo* root text says:

> Your body will be blissful, your speech melodious, your
> mind still, and you will accomplish immortality.§

Among the many explanations about the virtues of having
accomplished the vase-shaped breath, to summarize, are the ease
of having attained physical flexibility, melodiousness due to gaining
control over the voice, and that your mind can remain unmovingly
in samadhi, in addition to the accomplishment of the rasayana of
immortality. The *Samvarodaya Tantra* mentions this:

> Alternatively, by means of the *kumbhaka* practice,
> Everyone attains victory over death.

The Practice During Breaks

The *Lamrim Yeshe Nyingpo* root text says:

> In the session breaks do yogic exercises and rest peacefully.§
> At times, practice stillness of mind through vajra
> recitation.§

During all the breaks between the sessions of exerting yourself in this prana yoga, you should eliminate flaws pertaining to the
channels and energies with techniques such as the five-branch training; the discipline of the body and hitting the key points; and guiding, reversing, and distributing to the time of the bindus. Throughout
all of these, you should perform the yogic exercises in accordance
with the practical tradition to remove hindrances and bring forth
progress.⁴⁶

At the end, allow your three doors to remain at ease, as their dis-
turbances and the channels or energies will naturally be cleared. At
all times in between bring forth enhancement by means of the vajra
recitation and training in mental stillness. In general, the vajra rec-

itation is at all times of great importance, so we will elaborate a little upon its meaning with a quote from the *Heruka Galpo*:[47]

> The recitation to be applied as path
> While entering, remaining, and emerging
> Should be practiced with six aspects complete,
> And so you apply the vajra recitation.

The six aspects mentioned here correspond in meaning to the six yogas explained in the *Exposition Tantra Vajra Garland*. Among them, the first is the yoga of counting, which means to focus the attention on keeping track of the number of circulations until one can count all 21,600.[48]

Second, the following yoga is to be aware of the following of the four other elements for every energy occurrence, when the 2,700 circulations move during each of the eight sessions. Thus this is its clarifying aspects.

Third, the yoga of placing is to be aware of each of the areas through which the energies of inhalation and exhalation move. One knows that this is moving through such-and-such channel wheel, so that one focuses the attention on the manner of a sphere from the crown of the head to the soles of feet.

Fourth, the yoga of realizing thoughts is to be aware of the characteristics of the energies that add up to 21,600 and of the energies pertaining to the 108 energies of thoughts, consisting of the twenty energies of the five elements of the four chakras, which become multiplied tenfold when adding the left and right mandalas, so that you know the thoughts that are produced. By letting them become nonthought the very moment they arise, you are also aware of how thoughtfree wakefulness manifests. In this way you understand the flawless virtues pertaining to thought and nonthought.[49]

Fifth, the yoga of transformation is when the circulation of the previous thoughts' force reverts so that the 108 thought-energies turn into energies of nonthought, and they remain exclusively nonconceptual in equanimity. Nevertheless, when they circulate through the channels and chakras, they do have the taint of disturbing emotions and so are therefore called klesha energies or relative. When interrupted, they dissolve into the indestructible, and they're called wisdom energies or ultimate. Once more, they circle as before, to rise and circulate through the channel wheels, and so forth.

Sixth, the yoga of total purity is when, having transcended the distinctions of the energies circulating or not circulating through the channel wheels, they perpetually dissolve into the indestructible, so that the reality of the energies is the state of equanimity endowed with the characteristics of being clear, empty, and blissful. Thus, you remain evenly composed in luminosity during which all energies have dissolved within that state.

The way to apply the vajra recitation endowed with these six aspects is described in the *Prophecy of Realization*:[50]

> With utterance, and endowed with focus,
> The symbolic, and the ultimate.

In this way the vajra recitation is described as having four aspects. Even though there are many ways to explain their meaning, the general way to practice is the following. To recite verbally the three syllables is the vajra recitation with utterance. To visualize the three syllables in a form with shape and color is the vajra recitation with focus. To recite while recognizing that energy and mantra are indivisible, by imagining that the wind-energy and emerging, entering, and remaining are the manifestation of the three syllables, is the symbolic vajra recitation. To realize that names, words, and utterances are all like a magical illusion, while understanding that the coming, going, and remaining of the breath-energy are indivisible from the *mahamudra* of empty form, is regarded as the ultimate vajra recitation.[51]

Training the Essence Bodhichitta

Third, training in the bindus has two aspects: the principal part of the path and the subsidiary aspects of the path.

The Principal Part of the Path

This has two topics: explanation of the tummo of heat, of bliss, and of nonthought, and a summary of the meaning of these in terms of how they relate to the four aspects of Approach and Accomplishment.

Explanation of the Tummo of Heat, of Bliss, and of Nonthought

For the first, the *Lamrim Yeshe Nyingpo* root text says:

> Having become practiced in that, beneath the nirmana
> wheel⁚
> Is the concealed natural form of knowledge, *Chandali.*⁚
> Visualize the A stroke and kindle it, inciting it with the
> energies.⁚
> Entering the central pathway, invoke the deities of the
> wheels.⁚
>
> The blissful essence from the HANG at the crown of the
> head⁚
> Reinvigorates it, and again it blazes more and more.⁚
> By the channels and elements being filled with heat and
> bliss,⁚
> Actualize nonconceptual wisdom and bring it to the space
> of dharmata.⁚

After having grown familiar with these yogas of the channels and energies, visualize the wisdom fire of tummo, the pristine bindu or *Chandali*, which is the natural form of the hidden aspect of Prajnaparamita Yogini, approximately four fingers below the wheel of emanation at the navel.[52] Her shape is in the form of the A-*she*. The color is red and the touch is hot. The identity is empty, while the experience has the nature of bliss. In addition, visualize the syllable HANG at the upper end of the central channel, either as the actual letter or as the bindu endowed with the four characteristics—clear, brilliant, shiny, and rolled up.[53]

Provoked by the vase-shaped breath-energy together with the fourfold application, the flame grows to the size of about four fingers and gradually grows longer.[54] Moving through the hollow pathway of the central channel, it incites the unified deities of the channel bindus at the navel and the other three wheels. Finally, it touches the HANG at the crown of the head, so that bindus in a blissful stream appear, like a gentle rain or like the stalk of a fruit. When it dissolves into the tummo at the navel, the flame is invigorated, just like replenishing a butter lamp with liquid oil. And now the flame blazes larger and larger, so that it intermingles with the bliss that provokes bodhichitta. By so doing, it gradually spreads through the four chakras to permeate even the smallest channels in the body. Filled with warmth and bliss, the view of recognizing them to be equal taste as the identity of self-knowing, makes the non-conceptualizing wakefulness fully realized. During all three of the experiences in which the melting bliss has gained strength, in the end, without fixating on them as being of particular importance, you should bring them to the natural luminosity of primordial purity, the basic space of dharmata.[55]

Concerning the general points of tummo, the *Tantra of Being Equal to Space* describes three types: the natural as the outer, the A-*tung* as the inner, and the union as the secret type of tummo. Among these, the identity of the inner type of tummo, which is being cultivated in this context, is the inner *yogini*, the coemergent wisdom of blissful emptiness. The *Vajra Garland* describes her as follows:[56]

> Always present at the center of the navel,
> The light equal to a thousand suns
> Brings forth the flame of great wisdom.

As for the literal definition, the word *chandali* means wrathful, fierce, or burning, since whenever the key point is applied, it quickly consumes by fire the impurities of the aggregates and elements as well as thoughts and emotions.

As for its nature, due to the various intents of the sections of tantra, it is explained to be present as fire, wind, channel, essence, mantra, or wisdom. The general understanding is that it is the relative bindu, which is present as ultimate wisdom.[57]

The three factors which put it ablaze are the kindling of wind with the vase-shaped breath, and so forth; the focus on the seed syllable, attribute, fire bindu, A-she,[58] or the like; and the utilization of the method of either one's own or another's body.

As for the degree of blazing, there are three levels of blazing— lesser, middling, and greater—related to the energies of the roma and kyangma respectively entering, remaining, or dissolving into the central channel.

In terms of divisions, there are three other types of tummo: karma, yogini, and coemergent. Alternatively, these three are explained as the tummo of blazing, samaya, and heat; the tummo of melting, Dharma, and bliss; and the tummo of the experience of mingling, wisdom, and nonthought.[59]

In terms of measuring signs of progress, tummo causes the ten outer and inner signs, as well as causing both types of accomplishments of qualities.[60]

Summary of the Meaning of These in Terms of How They Relate to the Four Aspects of Approach and Accomplishment

For the second, the *Lamrim Yeshe Nyingpo* root text says:

The Approach and Full Approach of this profound
    development stage
Are the energy practices together with the yogic exercises.

By the Accomplishment of *Chandali,* you will realizeᵉ
The Great Accomplishment of undivided bliss and
    emptiness.ᵉ

The profound development stage devoid of artifice, explained
here, is the Approach. The Full Approach is the prana yoga, together
with the yogic exercises for training the body. Following that, by
means of the sequences for accomplishing the blazing and dripping
tummo, you realize the nature of the Great Accomplishment, which
is indivisible bliss and emptiness. In this way, without depending
upon a path involving elaborations, such as the layout of the mandala, you perfect the four aspects of Approach and Accomplishment
on the inner vajra path.

28

The Subsidiary Parts of the Path of the Secret Empowerment

The explanation of the subsidiary aspects of the path has two points: the brief statement and the detailed explanation.

THE BRIEF STATEMENT

The *Lamrim Yeshe Nyingpo* root text says:

As subsidiaries of this path,ᵉ

I shall now progressively teach the instructions that link together the yogas for day and night that are of utmost importance as subsidiary aspects of the path.

THE DETAILED EXPLANATION

The second has two parts: the yogas for daytime and the yogas for nighttime.

The Yogas for Daytime

The *Lamrim Yeshe Nyingpo* root text says:

Regard all daytime post-meditations as subsidiaries of this path,ᵉ
Impurely, as the eight analogies of illusion,ᵉ

And purely, as only mind, the apparent-empty form of the
     deity.§

Delight in the magical bliss of the path of learning by
     emerging§

In the mudra of mind-energy, and of the union of the path
     of no learning.§

The tummo yoga of melting bliss purifies the obscurations of the
channels, and the occasions of union and transference, and since it
generates coemergent wisdom, it is the life pillar of the path. One
should therefore make it the main part of the meditation practice.
During post-meditation, one should train in the yogas of day and
night according to one's individual fortune.

To explain, the illusory body purifies the situation of ordinary
delusion during the daytime post-meditation. Even though the
main objective to be accomplished is the illusory body of the hidden
meaning, prior to that one should train one's mind in the samadhi of
magical illusion. As a summary, it has the following four aspects.[61]

FIRST, THE IMPURE ILLUSORY BODY refers to all the entities
belonging to the vessels and contents of the three realms. You should
recognize that they are like the eight metaphors for magical illusion—experienced while nonexistent and devoid of true existence.[62]
The eight analogies are the following:

Magical illusion: devoid of true existence yet still perceived as
possessing the components of functioning completely.

Dream: appearing as mind only when distorted by confusion.

Visual aberration: not existing anywhere, neither inside nor outside, because of possessing no materiality.

Mirage: moving from moment to moment.

Reflection of the moon in water: one single [reflection] can be
present wherever.

Echo: arising and ceasing momentarily due to causes and conditions.

City of gandharvas: visible and yet unpredictable.

Magical apparition: appearing as one or many.

Similar to these eight analogies of illusion, all the phenomena of samsara and nirvana are endowed with an illusory body—they fully appear while being empty—and, therefore, this is the illusory body of the general meaning that is common to the literal meaning and to the meaning in the sutras.

SECOND, THE PURE ILLUSORY BODY means that all these present appearances do not have any separate existence apart from arising merely as the formations of mind, and that this mind as well is regarded, since the beginning, as the form of the deity that is the self-existing unity of appearance and emptiness. This perspective is also described in the *Five Stages*:

> The reflected image in a mirror
> Illustrates the body of magical illusion.
> Its colors, like those of the rainbow
> Are pervasive, like the moon in water.

THIRD, THE ILLUSORY BODY OF UTTER PERFECTION means that the energies dissolve into the central channel provoking the three or four levels of emptiness, so that at the end of either, the full attainment of that, all the luminosity emerges in the form of the deity in an instant from merely the mind-energy. After growing repeatedly familiar with this type of dissolving and reemerging, the hidden meaning is to accomplish the unity of the stage of training through emerging in the mudra form of wisdom, which is made from merely the mind-energy.[63]

FOURTH, THE ULTIMATE ILLUSORY BODY is, by having perfected this, the unity of the level of no training, which is completely free of defilement, and enjoys the bliss that is like a magical illusion, the domain of wisdom.

About this the *Galpo* says:

> The resultant self-consecration
> Is an illusion, like the moon in water,
> Or a rainbow, devoid of substance.
> Appearing in the resultant form like this
> Is adorned with the major and minor marks.

The Yogas for Nighttime

The second has two parts: the composure and the post-meditation.

The Composure

For the first, the *Lamrim Yeshe Nyingpo* root text says:

> Having realized the nature of all phenomena to be
>   emptiness and luminosity,[§]
> At the time of sleep, meditate evenly on the indestructible
>   bindu at the center of the heart.[§]
> By leading through the experiences of the four stages of
>   emptiness,[§]
> The example and meaning luminosities will effortlessly
>   dawn.[§]

Luminosity that purifies the defilement of the state of deep sleep also has four levels. The first is the literal meaning and the meaning that is common to the sutras. This is that the nature of all phenomena comprised of samsara and nirvana are devoid of the limits of mental constructs since the beginning, and therefore they are empty of identity while being unobstructedly perceptible in every possible way. Through stabilizing the samadhi in which this is recognized to be as it is, the energies dissolve into the central channel so that you are capable of reaching the four levels of emptiness.

Based on this, the second level is capturing the luminosity that is general to Mantrayana. Here, the key point of time is to practice in the early morning when sleep is light. The key point of body is to assume an upright posture; the determination is to be mindful of the moment of falling asleep; the key point of object is to remain in the composure in which the attention is focused one-pointedly on the pure essence of the heart center, which is the indestructible bindu. With this as the circumstance, you form the experience because, when the mind-and-energy comes together slightly and dissolves into the central channel, the signs that the elements successively dissolve will be experienced, such as the subtle experiences of smoke and so forth.[64]

The consciousness dissolving into appearance means that coarse conceptual states cease so that you experience the whiteness that resembles moonlight, the empty. Appearance dissolving into increase means that subtle thought states cease so that you experience the redness that resembles sunlight, the extremely empty. When increase dissolves into full attainment, thought states for the most part have ceased so that you experience the blackness, which resembles total darkness, the great empty. Full attainment dissolving into luminosity means that the totality of the mind-energy has ceased so that your experience is like the morning sky at autumn, free from the three kinds of interference, the totally empty. At the stages of each of these four levels of emptiness, you should identify them and, in particular, sustain the state of luminosity of the fourth for as long you can.

Third is the hidden meaning. When you have brought forth the continuity of this experience in the manner of joining day and night, you will attain mastery over the luminosity of example, distinguished by a certain degree of density and experience and realization at the time of the path of action.

With that as the cause, you will effortlessly experience the fourth, which is the ultimate luminosity of perfection. Thus, bringing death into the path as the *dharmakaya,* you will mingle the mother and child luminosities and make the differentiation within the primordial ground in a single instant.

The Post-Meditation

For the second, the *Lamrim Yeshe Nyingpo* root text says:

> In the post-meditation, through the force of aspiration and
>   energy practice,§
> Recognize dreams and train in the great skill of
>   transforming apparitions.§
> Dissolve into the state of great emptiness, and as the
>   illusory manifestation of compassion,§
> Accomplish the single and elaborate mudras and the group
>   assemblies filling the space.§

During the post-meditation, when training is about to begin after having remained in the composure of the luminosity of deep sleep, you instantly emerge in the form of the deity that is the illusory body. If you are unable to do that, this is the instruction for training during the dream state.

Through the force of determination, incessantly reminding yourself that daytime appearances are all dreams, and through the force of applying the key points related to the energy practice of *pranayama,* you will experience the deep sleep at nighttime as luminosity. But if you are unable to do so, you should recognize it to be a dream as soon as the energies stray into the roma and kyangma and circulate in the channels at the throat center, so that the phenomena of double delusion arise in the body of habitual tendencies. As soon as that happens, recognize these phenomena as being dreams. You should form the strong intention to do so.[65]

When you have become stable in this, you should make magical apparitions, such as bringing many from one and appearing in whichever way is necessary to influence beings. Once you have grown stable in that as well, you should transform and multiply entities in unpredictable and variegated ways, and so forth. Train in this until you perfect the great strength of the samadhi of dreaming.[66]

After perfecting this strength, dissolve all the phenomena of the double delusion into the continuity of great emptiness, and from within that state reemerge in the single-mudra form of the deity, which is formed out of mind-energy, as the natural manifestation of its magical compassion. Here, innumerable mudra forms emanate from you, and, at the end, clusters of deities emanate to fill the ends of space. To train diligently until you are capable of this is the way to fully complete dream practice as endowed with the four branches of Approach and Accomplishment. This will presently revert the clinging to the reality of deluded phenomena, and ultimately you will realize the bardo as being *sambhogakaya*.

Instructions in the Practice for the Moment of Death and the Bardo

The second has two parts: connecting with the above by stating the purpose and explaining these two individually.

Connecting with the Above by Stating the Purpose

The *Lamrim Yeshe Nyingpo* root text says:

> If you have not perfected the training within this lifetime,[§]

The lazy type of person who, even though he has received the pith instructions and engaged in the practice, does not attain the confidence of realization within this lifetime and has not brought forth the reality of familiarization should practice these instructions in order to perform the ejection of consciousness to the wisdom above at the time of death, to reconnect with the interruption of the path, and to perform the mingling with the three kayas in the bardo.

Explaining These Two Individually

The second has two parts: the practice at the time of death and the practice of the bardo.

The Practice at the Time of Death

For the first, the *Lamrim Yeshe Nyingpo* root text says:

> Gather mind-energy, eject, and rest in that state.§

To explain this, three types are generally taught: the foremost transference into the state of luminosity, the ultimate truth of the death state; the middling transference into the deity form of the illusory body, the correct relative truth of the bardo state; and the lesser transference within the development stage. Among these three, I shall here explain the latter so that you can put it to use at the time of death, having thoroughly trained in it while you are alive.[67]

For the physical key points and energy practice, block the nine doors to samsara, open the single door of liberation, dissolve the mind-energy into the support within the central channel either at the navel or at the heart, and eject and descend through the aperture of Dharma either with support or without, whichever is suitable. Once you are well trained in this, when the time comes and the signs of dying are complete, and there is no escaping by means of methods for fooling death, with one-pointed determination you should eject your consciousness into basic space so that you rest in the state of primordial purity that transcends thought and description.[68]

By doing so, the foremost result is to journey to the pure celestial realms so that you can attain the supreme accomplishment after completing the remaining part of the path. The middling result is to attain accomplishment by taking the support of the Mantrayana practitioner and continuing on to a pure rebirth. The lesser result is explained to be connecting with liberation gradually after taking rebirth in the higher realms and reconnecting with the path.

The Practice of the Bardo

For the second, the *Lamrim Yeshe Nyingpo* root text says:

> Join together by mixing the sights, sounds, and thoughts of
> the bardo⁣§
> With deity, mantra, and the great wisdom.§

If you fail to recognize the luminosity of the reverse order at the time of death, the progressive order appears, including full attainment manifesting from the totally empty and so forth, and the eighty innate thought states arise. When this happens, the mental body comprised of the four name aggregates is formed and you experience the deluded phenomena of the bardo.

This is the time to remind yourself of the key points of previous instructions and to recognize that deluded phenomena are unreal. By so doing, you should mingle perceived objects, the sounds heard, and the myriad thoughts—these three—with the deity of visible emptiness, the mantra of audible emptiness, and the great wisdom of aware emptiness.[69] Furthermore, in harmony with your former training, you should mingle them in the way that corresponds to the empowerments that ripen, the paths that liberate, the samayas to be observed, and the fruition to be attained. This will cause you to attain a *nirmanakaya* rebirth by connecting with a pure realm, and so forth.[70]

The person of the very lowest capacity should form an intense determination and bring forth deeply felt devotion, compassion, and renunciation, and so forth, through which he will block the door to the womb of an inferior place of rebirth.

The Second Principle Point, Linking with the Substitute for these with Other Paths: How Other Paths Are Included and the Result

The *Lamrim Yeshe Nyingpo* root text says:

> In this way, channels and essences are the deities of
> undivided samaya and wisdom.§

Through the threefold self-existence, visualization, and
   training,§
Take the wisdoms of enlightened body, speech, and mind as
   the path.§
Prana-union is empowerment and vajra-recitation.§
Make offerings with the chandali fire and praises with the
   song of the blazing and dripping.§
Within the pleasant assembly hall permeated by warmth,§
Delight in the feast and torma of the enjoyments of melting
   bliss.§
Dissolve in the state of nonthought and emerge as the
   illusory form of the deity.§
Reverse order is the space of luminous suchness.§
Progressive order is the all-illuminating and the cloud of
   the seed- syllable.§
By training in the skill of the single and elaborate forms in
   dreams,§
And through the group-gathering practice of undivided
   mind-energy,§
As the maturation, the three doors will be transformed into
   the three vajras,§
And the supreme siddhi of the three kayas spontaneously
   present as birth, death, and bardo,§
Will be naturally manifest without effort.§

Simply by means of the completion stages that are self-consecration taught here, you will also perfectly complete the path of the
first stages.

To explain this, the fundamental body's primary channel constituents are the chief and attending deities of the indivisibility of
samaya and wisdom. They are visualized by acknowledging them to
be the mandala of the vajra body that is formed in a self-existing
manner.

By means of the threefold maintaining of channels, energies, and essences, you take wisdom as the path in the sense of consecrating the three doors to be the vajra body, speech, and mind. Through binding the upper and lower energies in union, the empowerments are conferred and the vajra recitation of exhalation, inhalation, and remaining is uninterrupted.

The fire of tummo held at the navel makes offerings, and the natural sounds of the delightful bindu, blazing and dripping, and the indestructible, offer the praises of vajra songs. Within the joyful feast mansion of the body, permeated with the warmth of *chandali*, with great satisfaction you enjoy the melting bliss of the AH HANG, the feast and torma of undefiling nectar, after which you dissolve into the nonconceptualizing state of luminosity.

Once more, you reemerge as the threefold mandala—the illusory nature of the vessel and contents—which is the natural radiance of the deity's bodily form, the magical illusion of unity. Through this, during the two yogas of composure and post-meditation in the waking state, all possible elaborate activities are complete.

Dissolving the reverse order of the three experiences into luminosity, to remain in that state is the great emptiness of suchness. From that basic space, you manifest the reverse order during the post-meditation, which is the magical illusion of the all-illumination and the cloud of letters of the causal seed syllable.

Next, you manifest as the single-mudra form of the deity during the dream state, and by training the strength of the elaborate mudra forms, you manifest the great assembly that emanates infinite clusters of deities, which are undivided mind-and-energy.

By means of the yogas of composure and post-meditation during the sleep state, endowed with the four aspects of Approach and Accomplishment, the impure three doors of maturation are shifted or transformed into being the utterly pure three vajras: vajra body, vajra speech, and vajra mind.

With rebirth as nirmanakaya, death-state dharmakaya, and the bardo as sambhogakaya, the three phases of existence are spontaneously perfected as the nature of the three kayas. Hence, you will naturally and effortlessly experience the supreme accomplishment of true awakening.

29

The Practice of the Wisdom-Knowledge Empowerment

Third, the explanation of the practice of the wisdom-knowledge empowerment has three parts: connecting with a brief statement, a detailed explanation of that, and the conclusion of the topic.[71]

CONNECTING WITH A BRIEF STATEMENT

The *Lamrim Yeshe Nyingpo* root text says:

> When your experience and realization in any of these have
> greatly increased,§
> Then, for the practice of the wisdom-knowledge
> empowerment,§
> The stages of the Accomplishment of great bliss,§

When the strength of your experience and realization have greatly increased and progressed by means of having understood and grown accustomed to any of these yogas of meditation state and post-meditation—including authentic accomplishment in the energies and possessing the confidence of nontransference, which are the basis for the practices of self-consecration—then, the time has arrived for the practice of the third empowerment, the wisdom-knowledge empowerment:

> ... Through the mudra, sign deity of Great Attainment of
> Prophecy,§

You reach to the end of the Perfection of the Great
   Strength of abandonment and attainment,§
And your experience becomes of one taste with that of the
   Heruka.§

THE NOTES

PART 3
Entering the Path of Wisdom

A Supplemental Ornament to *The Light of Wisdom*—
The Commentary on the *Lamrim Yeshe Nyingpo,* the Oral
Instructions of Padma—
A Background Teaching for the Unexcelled Inner Three Tantras,
Compiled as Mnemonic Notes from the Oral Teachings of the
Lineage Masters,
Entitled *Entering the Path of Wisdom*

by Jamyang Drakpa *as recorded by* Jokyab Rinpoche

Supplemented with clarifying remarks
by Kyabje Dilgo Khyentse,
Kyabje Tulku Urgyen Rinpoche,
and other lineage masters

NOTE ATTRIBUTIONS

AB	Alex Berzin
EC	Elizabeth Calahan
Ed.	Editor, Marcia Schmidt
EPK	Erik Pema Kunsang
GA	Gyurme Avertin
JR	Jokyab Rinpoche
JV	Jim Valby
KYG	Khenpo Yonten Gyamtso
RB	Richard Barron
WF	Wulstan Fletcher

NOTES

1. The body mandala, as taught in the *Yumkha* sadhana is as follows: *The Eight Earthly Sacred Places (gocharya) of the Cycle of Speech*—the chakra of wealth (i.e., the throat) is *Lampaka*, the underarms and kidney cavity are *Kamarupa*, the two nipples are *Odra*, the navel is *Trishakuni*, the tip of the nose is *Koshala*, the palate is the country of *Kalinga*, the heart is *Kancika*, and Himalaya—and *the Eight Subterranean Sacred Places (bhugarbha)* of *the Cycle of Body*—the genitals are the land of *Pretapuri*, the anus is the land of *Grihadeva*, the thumbs and big toes are *Maru*, the thighs are *Saurashtra*, the calves are *Suvarnadvipa*, the sixteen fingers and toes are *Nagara*, the knees are *Kulanta* and *Sindhu*. Jigme Lingpa, *Yumkha Dechen Gyalmo, Queen of Great Bliss*, Rigpa, Translated by Tulku Thondrub, edited by Adam Peacey, 2012, Page 60.

2. The Tibetan words for "center" (*dkyil*) and "circle" (*'khor*) combined form the word for "mandala" (*dkyil 'khor*). [EPK]

3. The *Magical Key to the Treasury* is found in *The Hundred Thousand Nyingma Tantras*, volume 2, Text number 24. [EPK]

4. The subtle body, speech, and mind are the subtle aspects of channels, energies, and essences, as well as the subtle obscurations of the three doors in the particular case of bodhisattvas on the path who have attained the bhumis.

   The six families are the five families plus Vajrasattva's family. Furthermore, the cause is Akshobhya, the result is Vajrasattva or Vajradhara, the pervader is the victorious ones of the five families, and the pervasive aspect is the embodiment of all families—Vajrasattva or Vajradhara.

   The five primary elements are the five families. Consciousness is Vajrasattva.

   Furthermore, regarding the three bodies—gross, subtle, and extremely subtle—body channels can be impure and absolutely pure. In other words, the characteristics that define beings in samsara, beings having set upon the path, and nirvana, as can be drawn from the *Sublime Continuum* (v. 47):

The three stages of impurity,
Impurity purified, and absolute purity,
Are called respectively sentient beings,
Bodhisattvas, and *tathagatas*. [JR]

5. The gross aspects are body, speech, and mind; the subtle aspects
are the channel, energies, and essences; and the extremely subtle
are semen, ovum, and wind. Alternatively, the gross aspects are the
body, speech, and mind of the three realms; the subtle, the three
doors of shravakas, pratyekabuddhas and bodhisattvas; and the
extremely subtle, buddhas' body, speech, and mind. [JR]

6. Avadhuti means "all-vibrating" or "duality relinquisher." Further,
"all-vibrating" means "all-pervasive," while "duality relinquisher"
indicates that it relinquishes all dualistic clinging to subject and
object. "Central channel" means it doesn't lean towards either the
kyangma or roma channels. It is also called the "single mulberry
tree" (*tshangs pa'i shing gcig*). *Lala* (Skt.) refers to the roma (Tib.)
channel, and *rasa* (Skt.) to the kyangma (Tib.). The kyangma channel generates the body, the roma the speech, and the central channel
the mind. Based on that, the white and red appearances manifest
outwardly as day and night, inwardly as well-being and suffering,
and in between as desire and aversion. Duality of subject and object
arises as these three pairs. These two aspects can be referred to in
these different ways interchangeably. [JR]

7. The roma, kyangma, and central channels meet under the navel.
Then they are bound together at the navel as if with an iron chain.
The three channels are present individually just before the central
channel reaches the heart, and they merge into one at the heart and
likewise at the throat and the crown of the head.

      According to Jamyang Khyentse Wangpo, this also explains the
phrase, "The channels bound as if with an iron chain. . ." The knots
of the channels are not tight knots but loose ones—the term "knot"
is applied to the bending of the channels towards each other. [JR]

8. "The twelve channels of transition" are the inner level. Externally,
they are the twelve houses of the sun and the related sheep, ox, and
so on. [JR]

9.   For the sixty-four channels at the center of the chakra, see the diagram on the following page. [JR]

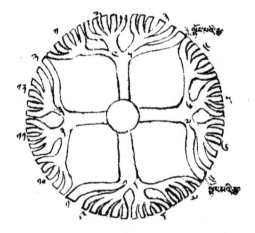

Diagram 1

Exhaustion, dissolution, nonvirtue
Sun, wind, expelling   I,!
   IH killing   !
----------------------   !
Fire element   !
RIH! Kalagni planet! Water
   element
Mars! All activities! Jupiter
Summon! except killing!

Magnetize- LEEH Saturn

earth element/Stun and paralyze-!
RIGHT NOSTRIL

Increase, arising, positivity
I wind element, moon-!
Expelling, killing-!
RI!
AH   !UH   Me! U! A RAHU! Fire !
Water element! Accomplish!
   Mercury
! Venus! All activities! Summon
Pacifying and! Pacifying and ! !
   Magnetize
enriching! Enriching-LEE earth
   element!
Conclusion, stun and paralyze!
LEFT NOSTRIL

10. The channels at the navel are the first ones to form, and the entire network of channels unfolds from them. So this is the crucial point of the unity of the outer, inner, and other aspects. [JR]

The outer, inner and other aspects are as previously mentioned: "the white and red appearances manifest outwardly as day and night, inwardly as well-being and suffering, and in between as desire and aversion." [KYG, GA]

11. In general the twenty-four sacred places and the thirty-seven hallowed lands are introduced in the teachings of the Sarma and Nyingma schools, and in particular they can be found in the *Profound Inner Topics*. Especially if you want to get to the bottom of it, you need to consult the *Profound Inner Topics*, which presents them with precision. According to Jamyang Khyentse Wangpo, this commentary brings up all the essential points and explains them very well. [JR]

Jamgön Kongtrül gives a list of these twenty-four sacred places (*gnas nyer bzhi*) in his *Commentary on Sangtik Yumkha:* Jalandhara at the crown of the head, Pulliramala between the eyebrows, Arbuta at the nape, Rameshvara in the middle of the eyebrows, Oddiyana in the right ear, Godavari in the left ear, Devikoti in the two eyes, Mallava on the shoulders, Lampaka in the throat, Kamarupa in the armpits, Otri in the breasts, Trishakune in the navel, Koshala in the tip of the nose, Khakalinga at the heart, Kanchika and Himalaya, in the upper arm, Pretapuri in the sexual organ, Grihadeva in the anus, Maruta in the thumbs, Saurashta in the thighs, Suvarnadvipa in the calves, Nagara in the fingers, Kuluta in the knees, and Sindhu in the upper part of the foot. [EPK]

12. Please notice that *rlung* is mainly translated as "energy" or "energies" here. Other choices include "wind-energies," "winds," "currents," and so on. [EPK]

13. The "causal tantra" or "causal continuum" refers to the ground continuum or buddha nature, which is the support. What are supported are the all-ground consciousness and the other seven collections of consciousness. The life-upholding energy corresponds to the consciousness, the upward-moving energy to form, all-pervading to sensation, fire-accompanying to perception, and downward-clear-

ing to formation. The five energies can also be related to the five primary elements: life-upholding and space; upward-moving and wind; all-pervading and water; fire-accompanying and fire; and downward-clearing and earth. [JR]

14. "They do not descend into the mandala" means they do not descend into the element. [JR]

15. The elements do not descend or move into the four empty channels of the navel. [JR]

16. The "half hour" refers to a period of 22½ minutes. [JV]

"Expansion" refers to the energies emerging from the navel and expanding to the pores. When they return (retraction) they also dissolve into the navel.

The primary elements are destroyed one after the other, dissolving into the right nostril. The left nostril is the place where the four primary elements progressively arise. They arise during the waxing moon and dissolve during the waning phase of the moon.

There is transfer from one chakra channel to another every half hour or every five periods. Six breaths are one period [*chu tshod*], and sixty periods are one time measure [*cho srang*]; sixty time measures correspond to one day. The subtle constituents of the body are preserved through seven lifetimes. There are long (eight), medium (sixteen) and short (thirty-two) spans: The four parts of day and the four parts of night taken together form the eight long spans, and you can calculate the others applying the same formula.

For example, earth energy is subdivided into a complete set of the four primary elements each having a corresponding energy. It is the same for the other element energies. [JR]

For a little more detail on these time divisions, see the section "Time" in Mipham Rinpoche, *Khenjuk*, vol. 1, Rangjung Yeshe Publications, 1997, Pages 81-85. The statement that the subtle constituents of body are preserved through seven lifetimes contradicts the teaching that the body ceases at death. These constituents are elements of the body, not consciousness, which is what continues on to the next life. Besides, consciousness does not continue for just seven lifetimes, as it has been circling in samsara for time without beginning. [GA]

17. "Thirty-two divisions" means that each breath has thirty-two parts, and the four wisdom energies are present during one fourth of them: Thirty-two divided by four makes eight divisions. "Fifty-six fractions" should be understood in the same way.

Among the thirty-two parts of one breath, thirty-one are karmic wind-energy and one is wisdom wind-energy. The four wisdom wind-energies that travel in the four empty channels need to be counted as one.

This amounts to one period, fifty-two half hours, and three breaths. Writing down the calculation in a diagram would make it clear. You can also understand without a diagram if you calculate with precision. [JR]

18. Different translators have various interpretations for each of these measures of time and have offered their explanations through personal communication with me. (Ed)

Chu tshod: a division of time equal to four breaths. [JV]

For those of us Kalachakra nerds who like precision:

56.25 ye shes rlung/'pho ba x 12 'pho ba/day = 675 ye shes rlung/day.

675 ye shes rlung/day x 360 days/year = 243,000 ye shes rlung/year.

243,000 ye shes rlung/year x 100 years/life span = 24,300,000 ye shes rlung/100-year life span.

360 days/year x 3 years = 1,080 days/3 years.

Three phyogs (phases of the moon) = 45 days.

1,080 + 45 = 1,125 days/3 years and 3 moon phases.

1,800 breaths/'pho ba x 12 'pho ba/day = 21,600 breaths/day.

21,600 breaths/day x 1,125 days/3 years and 3 moon phases = 24,300,000 breaths/3 years and 3 moon phases.

24,300,000 ye shes rlung/100-year life span = 24,300,000 breaths/3 years and 3 moon phases. [AB]

There is further information about the winds in appendix 6 of *Treasury of Precious Qualities,* book 2, p. 359 ff. Khenpo Yonten Gyamtso comments: The winds related to consciousness have the nature of the wisdom wind. This is ultimately devoid of movement and is therefore said to remain in a condition of stillness. On the other hand, the *Kalachakra* states that, "The Wisdom wind moves once for every thirty-two and a half respirations." In an oral commentary on this passage, Dilgo Khyentse Rinpoche once remarked:

It is said that in one day, a healthy adult experiences 21,600 complete respirations, which means that the average length of a single breath is four seconds. For every 32½ respirations, there is one movement of the wisdom wind. Given that, in the present age, it is said that the limit of human life is one hundred years, the duration of the wisdom breaths taken in a single lifetime, when added together, comes to a total of three years and three months. This is the reason for the duration of the traditional three-year retreat. [WF]

There is quite a bit about this in Jamgön Kongtrül's commentary on the *Zab mo nang don*. I've given an overview of the correspondences between the different time measurements in appendix 3 in my translation of that text, and definitions of each term in the glossary

breath (*dbugs, liptā*). The basic unit for time measurement in the system used by *The Profound Inner Principles*. One breath is the length of time a healthy individual takes to inhale and exhale. Six breaths make up one pāṇīpala; 360 comprise one ghatikā, or danda; 1,800 breaths are called a lagna, or major sankrānti; and 21,600 breaths comprise one solar day.

danda (*dbyu gu*, "sticks"). Equivalent to a minor sankrānti and a ghatikā, or *nāḍī* (*chu tshod*, "water-measure"). According to Henning (2007, 12): [Danda] literally means stick, and this refers to an ancient Indian custom of beating a drum or gong with a stick to mark each nāḍī. A danda is equivalent to 360 breaths, or twenty-four minutes.

ghatikā (or *nāḍī, chu tshod*, "water-measure"). A time period equivalent to 360 breaths, or twenty-four minutes. It was measured by one of two types of ancient Indian water clocks (an outflow type or floating-bowl type). (See Fleet 1915.) There are sixty ghatikās in one solar day. There are occasions (or calculations) when lunar days are divided into sixty

ghatikās that are "slightly shorter in duration than those that
are sixtieth parts of a solar day." See Henning 2007, 268.
This term is also translated as "half-period," "hour," and "major
clepsydra measure." It is equivalent to a danda and a minor
sankranti.

pānīpala (*chu srang,* "water weights"). The period of time it takes
to breath in and out six times. Sixty pānīpalas make up one
ghatikā. One pānīpala is equivalent to twenty-four seconds.
Also translated as "minor clepsydra measure" [an ancient
time-measuring device worked by a flow of water]
and "interval." [EC]

19. "Three years" is easy to understand. "The three sections" correspond
to the two parts of a month: the white part in two sections, and the
red one, which makes three sections. [JR]

These three sections are, respectively, the 1st to the 10th day, the
11th to 20th, and the 21st to the 30th. [GA]

20. There are twelve fingers for the earth energy, and likewise thirteen
for water, fourteen for fire, fifteen for wind, and sixteen for space.
There is also a way of counting four fingers for each, according to
Jamyang Khyentse Wangpo. [JR]

21. The nature of the wind-energy—the life-supporting wind-energy in
the central channel—is as follows: In the center of the wheel with
eight channels at the heart, the all-ground consciousness appears
in the form of a syllable A, which is space in nature. The downward-clearing wind, which is the element earth, is a syllable LAM
at the junction of the three channels. The upward-moving wind,
the fire element, is a syllable RAM in the east. The fire-accompanying wind, the element wind, is a syllable AM in the southeast. The
all-pervading wind-energy, the element water, is a syllable U in the
south. These are the five root wind-energies.

Concerning the five secondary wind-energies, the *naga* wind-energy, the element earth, gives rise to the wisdom devoid of real
existence; it appears as a space syllable AH in the southwest and
corresponds to the eyes and the form. The turtle wind, the wind
element, is a syllable A in the west and corresponds to the ear and

sound. The lizard wind-energy, the element fire, in the northwest, is a syllable AHR corresponding to nose and smell. The Devadatta wind-energy, the water element, is an OM syllable in the north, corresponding to the tongue and taste. The *asura* wind-energy, the element earth, is a syllable AH in the east, corresponding to body and tactile sensation. [JR]

22. The explanation of the gross wind-energy is complete. The ten energies of expression are the five root and five secondary energies, which are like the mount of the mind animated by the different thoughts. They are the mount of the four visions, which are (1) appearance, (2) flaring, (3) attainment, and (4) full attainment. Specifically concerning the clear light, clear light comes after the full attainment. [JR]

23. The binding of wind-energies corresponds to the vajra recitation as explained in the father tantras and the vase recitation as practiced in the mother tantras, in other words, wind-energy and energy-bindu. [JR]

24. Above the tip of the nose are the hand implements of the deities and so on—forms of the deity, hand implements, and seed syllables. Under the tip of the nose is the secret place, and in between at the level of the nose is the heart. [JR]

25. The root energy-bindu, which is freedom from elaboration, has three aspects: nature, radiance, and display. The delusional energy-bindu of ignorance has three aspects: letter, wind-energy, and substance energy-bindus. Each of these is divided into the basis for purification and purifying agent, adding up to six aspects. The first is the twelve links of interdependent origination; the second, deity, meditation, and mantra recitation. The third is the impelling wind-energies; the fourth, the binding of wind-energies. The fifth, the energy-bindu of the red and white substances; the sixth, their binding.

The substance energy-bindus are the white and red substances; there are pure and impure ones, fundamental, and transferring. [JR]

26. Distinctions between the pure and the impure: (1) Moving in the *miche matsongma* channel (These channel names come from the medical tantras. KYG) are the elements like teeth and nails that are

hard and difficult to break. In this case, the name of the result has been given to the cause. (2) The *trazukma* channel connected to the aperture of Brahma at the top of the head is where the very subtle hair and body hair travel. (3) From the *namsel tsema* or *salwama,* comes the skin. (4) From the *taktsu yönma* channel on the left travels the flesh, or the pure left element. (5) In the *nayön tunguma* channel are small movements of water. (6) In the *rubel kyema* between the eyebrows transit the bones, which are hard like the shell of a turtle. (7) In the *gompamo* channel outside the eyes transits the flesh of the liver. (8) In the *tsawangma* channel in the two upper arms transits the flesh of the heart. (9) In the *kyonma* channel in the armpits transits the flesh of the eyeballs. (10) In the *jukma* channel of the breasts travel excrements, gall bladder in nature. (11) In the *mamo* channel at the navel transits the element that actually gives rise to the body, or lungs. (12) In the *zukpa tsenmo* channel at the tip of the nose transit the intestines. (13) In the *siljinma* channel of the mouth coolness or heat transit. (14) From the *tsawa* channel in the middle of the throat come warmth and the colon. These fourteen are pure wisdom in nature when the moon is waxing.

With skill-in-means based on the roma channel, during the waning moon, the ten pure channels are maintained in the lower part of the body: (15) From the *zholma* channel of the breasts, from the heart down to the anus, the excrements flow down. (16) From the *gangpa rangma* transits the spinal marrow. (17) Phlegm flows from the general lower gateway. [(18) is missing in the text.] (19) In the great channel of the thighs flow the intestines for the growth of the body. (20) From the *jinnyi jordralma* comes sweat. (21) From the *dugu* channels of the toes flows the blood essence that embellishes the body. (22) Sweat or saliva moves in the heel *drupmo* channels during intercourse. (23) In the *pukyil tsachema* in the big toes flow saliva and mucus. This is because most of the saliva in the face comes from pain. In the *nyenkong yizangma* channel in the knees flows the spit. It is called the "small extremity," since whenever it is released a small amount of bliss and well-being arises. These also correspond to Pullirama at the crown and so on. [JR]

27. Furthermore, dissolution is the past aspect; it is the transformation

into impurity after the full completion of the action. The enjoyment is the present, main, white aspect during the accomplishment of the activity based on the pure essence of the element. The producing agent is the root of both pure and impure aspects; it is the cause. So, it corresponds to the future aspect of the mixing of energy and blood.

Each of the twenty-four elements can be divided into three thousand, adding up to seventy-two thousand. There are twenty-four thousand main dissolving energies; twenty-four thousand enjoyment ones, becoming mainly the white aspect; and twenty-four thousand agents, becoming mainly the red aspect. They correspond to the three elements of sun, moon, and Rahu. They fill the channels in the body entirely to the extremity of the body hair. [JR]

28. The twenty-four great channels and the five channels that support the five secondary energies, together with the three main channels, add up to thirty-two. With the five channels that support the five root wind-energies, the tally is thirty-seven. [JR]

29. The summation corresponding to the section starting, "When binding these three to be unchanging," is as follows: There are five channels where the energy of the five faculties transit—the *sumkhor*, *d*öma, *khyima*, *tummo*, and *dudral* channels.

30. In the case of both male and female, when the white and red elements turn to either the right or the left, the *la*-supporting syllable moves through the body. [JR]

Semen, ovum, blood, obscuration, and energy. [JR]

31. "Examination and no examination" means to conduct an examination, and the absence of investigation.

The "clusters of the minor families": For example, the peaceful deities Vairochana *yabyum* who are the main deities of the major family, are surrounded by a retinue of minor family deities. In the intermediate directions there are Vajrasattva, Dorje Gyalpo, Dorje Chakpa, and the female Dorje Gekmo, Dorje Dukpa, Dorje Chakyu, and Dorje Drolma. The gatekeepers yabyum have ten wrathful ones, and so on.

It is the same for the wrathful deities—the main deities correspond to the major families. In the center around Buddha Heruka, for example, there is the retinue of deities of the minor families as follows: In the intermediate direction are the four herukas (Vajra, Ratna, Padma and Karma) and the four consort Vajra, Ratna, Padma, and Karma *krodhishorimas*—the ten wrathful ones yabyum. There are also the twenty gatekeepers from the places and lands, the twenty-eight *ishvaris*, and the twenty wrathful ones yabyum.

The retinue of Padma Heruka also is composed of the Teka, Kesha, Pesha, and Besha Herukas. These four herukas are in union with their consorts, Tesha Krodhishorima, and so on. They are the ten main and retinue deities. The other deities from the places and lands, and so on, are as above. The other families are to be understood in the same way. This is the teaching of the *Magical Net*. [JR]

32. "The sixteen aspects of the bindus" are as follows: On the crown of the head are the sixteen bindus whose essence is the sixteen joys. Half of these—eight—descend into the throat; half of these eight—four—descend into the heart; half of these four—two—descend into the navel; and half of these two—one—abides at the secret place. This is the meaning of the phrase, "the sixteen halved bindus," from the *Magical Net of Manjushri*. Know that there are many other ways to explain it. [JR]

33. "The four levels of emptiness" are empty, great empty, extremely empty, all empty. Their explanation comes later in the text. [JR]

34. Here "nada" refers to extremely subtle wind-energy free from any gross obscuration. The obscurations of the three realms are embodied in the channels. They cannot be eliminated before the end of the continuum but are removed by the vajra-like antidote. According to Jamyang Khyentse Wangpo, these very subtle obscurations are not without aspects, but these are extremely subtle ones. [JR]

35. "Outer, inner, and secret warmth": For the development practice, this has been explained clearly in Jamgön Kongtrül's text. The signs in dreams will be explained in the *dzogchen* section.

When the text says, "Training the structuring channels, the moving energies, and the essence-bodhichitta," the root of all the wisdom channels is the central channel, and the root of all the samasaric channels is the life force. The Rahu channel, in which these two aspects are indivisible, can also be called the channel of life force because it is the support for the life force. The root of all the wisdom energies is the indestructible energy, and the root of all the karmic energies is the great life-force energy. The Rahu energy in which these two energies are mixed like milk with water is also rightly called the life-force energy.

At the time of the ground, it is the central channel. At the time of the path—based on the entry of mind-energy into the central channel—it takes the external empty form of a black tube with a diameter the width of a hair and free from stain, emanating rays of light. At the time of the fruition, the unobscured nature abides in the central, supreme *vajrakaya*. [JR]

36. Longchen Rabjam here refers to one of the tantras from the Space Section. [JR]

37. According to Jamyang Khyentse Wangpo, "the extremity of the eyes, the tip of the nose, and the mind in tune means that the way one looks with the eyes and the way one holds the mind should be to focus, both of them on the tip of the nose, and they shouldn't be separate from each other. When the breath flows evenly through both nostrils, this is wisdom wind-energy. [JR]

38. The four characteristics are that it is (1) straight like the trunk of a plantain tree, (2) bright like a lamp burning sesame oil, (3) delicate like the petal of a lotus, (4) blue in color like oxidized copper. Alternatively, the fourth characteristic can be said to be that it is hollow like a bamboo. [JR]

39. The completely arrayed summit refers to the pinnacle configuration. [RB]

40 "The wheel of the generation at the navel has sixty-four spokes," which are arranged as follows: It is said that "If you familiarize yourself with visualizing them." In the way they progressively split up—in accordance with how they are—and in the visualization of their divisions that portray them, all the channels radiate from the center like spokes of an umbrella. [JR]

Nadi essay from *Gongpa Zangtal* explains these names.[EPK]

41. For the outer, inner, and secret circles, consult diagram 1 on page62. [JR]

42. "With skill in the key point concerning the timing of the energies . . .": The demon of the son of the gods abides in the eyes. It moves

at dawn and is accompanied by the monk demons. The sign of this is that you strongly want to go. Expel the foul air, and meditate on the lama in all the channels of the eyes.

The demon of the aggregates abides in the flesh and the bones. It moves at midday and is accompanied by the earth lords. The signs are heavy body elements. Expel the foul air, and mediate on the lama on top of your head.

The demon of destructive emotions abides in the semen and ovum. It moves in the evening and is accompanied by the female spirits. The sign is that desire arises. Expel the foul air, and meditate on the lama at the navel.

The demon of the lord of death abides in the life-force channel. It moves at midnight and is accompanied by the spirits of the dead. The sign is that fear comes. Expel the foul air and meditate on the lama at your heart. This is the teaching of the great accomplished master Karma Pakshi.

At such times, you should not retain the energies. Furthermore, when the five poisons like desire, aversion, or ignorance arise, do not retain the energies. When faith, pure perception, devotion, compassion, and the like arise, do not expel the foul air, but at that time retain the energies. There are many explanations regarding faults and qualities associated with these points, but I will not give further explanation in this context.

There are five situations when the energies should not be retained. Persons with wounds on their body should not retain the energies, as their wounds will not heal easily. Likewise, a woman who is pregnant should not retain the energies, as the delivery will be difficult. Old people who have difficulty controlling their breath should not retain the energies. Neuters do not have the qualities of the energies and so should also not retain them. Finally, when you have an illness of any sort, your humors are imbalanced, so do not retain the wind-energies.

Further times at which you should not retain the energies are when you are having difficulty recovering from tiredness; when you are sick and in great pain; when you have just woken up; when you are having intercourse, except when drawing and diffusing the energies [i.e., practicing tsa lung]; when fearing trouble and pain; when sated; or when in a smoky or dusty environment.

Do not retain the energies when they move through the right nostril, but do it when they move through the left. When the movement is even through both, the energy is wisdom wind, so it is excellent. [JR]

43. The four applications of filling like a vase, and so on, are the applications of energies from the mother tantras. These four applications are explained clearly in the text, and as it is said:

> If you are not clear about the four applications,
> Their qualities will turn into many problems.

Distributing outside in the pores of the skin; distributing inside in the expanse of the central channel. Furthermore, stack short inhalations, and also exert small pressure. [JR]

44. When the text says explicitly "to make one round with the palm of your hand touching each kneecap," this implies also the forehead. After you have touched all three, snap your finger once. This is the time measure you accumulate. [JR]

45. The five-branch training should be learned following the sequence in the texts.

Though there are many practices for eliminating obstacles, the two most profound ones are devotion and prayer. Though there are many ways of enhancing the practice, the most profound is diligence. Though there are many yogic exercises, the most profound is to maintain the key points of the body. Though there are many ways of retaining the energies, the most profound is in directing the practice. [JR]

46. Here the vajra recitation corresponds to the union of energies as explained in the father tantras. [JR]

47. The six aspects are counting, following, placing, realizing thoughts, transforming, and total purity. [JR]

48. The yoga of realizing thoughts: The energies pertaining to the 108 energies of thoughts can be illustrated by the three phases of arising, engagement, and rest, for example, and consist of the twenty energies of the five elements (earth, and so forth) of the four

chakras such as the navel chakra—twenty multiplied by 108 gives 21,600. On top of this, these energies are multiplied tenfold when adding the five left and five right mandalas of the elements of the right and left nostrils, so that one knows the thoughts that are produced. By being aware of any subtle and gross thought that arises and letting these mind-and-energies become the near attainment of nonthought the very moment they arise, one is also aware of how thoughtfree wakefulness manifests. In this way one understands clearly the difference between the flaws and the virtues pertaining to thought (negative emotions) and nonthought (primordial wisdom). [JR]

49. The Sanskrit title of the *Prophecy of Realization* is the *Sandhi Vyakarana*, the exposition tantra of the father tantra *Guhyasamaja*. [EPK]

50. Training in the shape of three syllables in the vajra recitation: At the junction of the three channels that you visualize clearly in the deity's body without the wheels at the center is an a-she that transforms into a sun mandala. Atop the sun visualize a red letter AH, which is by nature the enlightened speech of all the victorious ones. Meditate on the union in vase breathing: When you exhale, at the knot of silken threads endowed with the five rays of light of the five elements emerging from the syllable AH, visualize that a dark blue syllable HUNG emanates, which travels through the nose and comes to rest one arm-span in front of the nose. When you inhale, a white syllable OM with beams of light enters through your nose and dissolves into the AH syllable. When you hold the breath, focus your mind on the HUNG syllable outside and the AH inside.

Signs of the energy retaining practice are to see lights of the five colors in the nostril, and so on. If you cannot hold the energies in this way, you can do the samaya vajra recitation. To stabilize the retaining of the energies, just rely on the energies as you do the wisdom vajra recitation. In particular, do the vajra recitation within the indivisibility of samaya being and wisdom being. [JR]

51. The hidden form of the Prajnaparamita Yogini is the delightful *Chandali*. The symbol is tummo or *Chandali*, the meaning it refers to is emptiness, and the significance or correspondence is Varahi—

together, these are known as the three *varahis* or three yoginis. The defining characteristics of tummo are clear from the text. [JR]

52. For the HANG syllable at the upper end of the central channel also, the symbol is the letter HANG, the meaning is supreme bliss—the three herukas. Additionally, it has four characteristics: It is white like the autumn moon, bright like a lamp burning sesame oil, round like a bird's egg, and on the verge of melting like mercury. [JR]

53. The fourfold application has been explained clearly above. Here one draws like a hook, fills like a vase, binds like a knot, and shoots up like an arrow. [JR]

54. The three experiences in which the melting bliss has gained strength are the three empty experiences of bliss, clarity, and absence of thought or experience of the empty. [JR]

55. In the natural, outer tummo, all phenomena are emptiness by nature; the *tsanda*, the inner tummo, corresponds to the small A below; and the union, secret tummo, is the union of bliss and emptiness. *Chandali* is tummo. The fire drop is red in color, its contact is hot, its essence empty, its aspect bliss—this is the A-she of the navel. [JR]

56. The upside-down letter, in the avadhuti channel where the warmth of the energy is experienced, is a drop just the size of a chickpea, which is to say the size of a mustard seed. The mantra is the small A. Together with the bindu of unstained primordial wakefulness, the seed syllables A and RAM and the hand implement—which is the *phurba*—they are present in the practitioner's continuum. [JR]

57. The bindu fire and A-she are similar. Generally speaking, by holding the energy applying the different aspects of the practice, you will eliminate the 404 diseases. With the blazing, you overcome the 21,000 malevolent influences (*dön*). With the dripping bliss, you liberate the 84,000 destructive emotions. Combined with emptiness, you can obtain the supreme accomplishment in one lifetime.

58. Invoking the mandala deities,
Blazing of the fire, the tummo of warmth,
Contained in basic space.
    The practice is sealed with the tummo of nonthought. The measure of the blazing is when the energies of the roma and

kyangma first enter the central channel, in the middle they abide there, and at the end they dissolve into the expanse of the central channel. [JR]

59. The ten signs are the signs that basic space and primordial wakefulness have become one taste thanks to the entering of the mind-and-energy into the central. They are as follows: appearances that look like smoke, a mirage, clouds, sun, moon, a blazing jewel, Rahu, stars, or rays of light. Jamyang Drakpa Rinpoche said this was Jamyang Khyentse Wangpo's explanation. [JR]

60. Then, if the illustrative wisdom dawns in one's mind, in the post-meditation one is able to arise as what we call the impure illusory body, which in reality is the deity formed simply of mind-and-energy. If the absolute wisdom dawns in one's mind, one is able to arise as what is known as the pure illusory body, which is the deity that appears from the radiance of primal wisdom. [*zinbris,* which means note, assuming the same as above Jamyang Khyentse Wangpo's explanation. Ed.]

61. The impure illusory body: Generally speaking the sutras mention the eight similes of illusion. In general, all appearing things—self and other than self—are like an illusion. In particular the appearances of self, me, and mine, and all well-being and suffering are like a dream. "Other than self" refers to enemies, close relatives, or people in between, who are like optical illusions. Areas and the places one inhabits are like mirages. Wealth and possessions are like reflections of the moon in water. Resounding sounds of praise and criticism are like echoes. One's abode, bed, house, and family are like a gandharva city. Actions, actors, and objects are like magical illusions. This is the mind-training to be practiced.

The tantras speak of twelve analogies for magical illusion. The teachings on mixing and transference list sixteen. In India, the favored example was illusion, while in Tibet it is the dream. The twelve analogies for magical illusion in succession are as follows. The *Self-blessing* says:

Namely, illusion, mirage, gandharva city, the bow of
Indra [i.e., the rainbow], reflections in a mirror, the

moon in water, echoes, dreams, optical illusions, clouds, lightning, and water bubbles—these are the twelve analogies of illusion. [JR]

62. The illusory body of utter perfection: Entering and emerging the four empty channels enter the central channel at their extremities. The mudra of the deity arises once again by rising in the reverse way. The union of training relates to the ten bhumis, and the fourth, the union of no-training, to buddhahood.

"Union" refers to the unity of the kayas and wisdoms.

I will explain a little further the three aspects of appearance, increase, and attainment that are so crucial to the illusory body and other related practices. Naropa's *Primer* explains:

> Appearances dissolve and gross phenomena dissolve;
> Thoughts dissolve and subtle phenomena dissolve.
> After dissolution comes habituation,
> And the clear light nature will arise.
> After comes the unity of the kayas,
> Which has two aspects:
> Training and no-training.
> Once it has become no-training,
> We speak of "realization of the fruition."

Accordingly, the dissolution of appearances refers to the dissolution of the forms in the eyes, or of forms in sounds so that the eyes do not see forms. Sounds dissolve in the next objects [i.e., smells], which dissolve in the next objects, and so on, progressively. As a result, the ears cannot hear sounds, and so on: The five physical faculties are blocked, and appearances have dissolved.

Gross phenomena dissolve: When earth dissolves into water, the body losses its vitality; water dissolves into fire, and the mouth is dry; fire dissolves into wind, and the body heat faints; wind dissolves into consciousness, and breathing resorbs [absorbs again]. When the gross elements have dissolved, and the outer breathing stops but before the inner breathing is interrupted, the four clear lights arise one after the other in the following way:

1. Appearance dissolves into the increase. When the white element of the crown descends to the heart, the external sign is that it is as if the moon is rising; the inner sign is smokelike appearance. The thirty-three thoughts related to the transformation of anger cease.
2. The increase dissolves into the attainment. Then, when the red element below the navel travels to the heart, the external sign is as if the sun is rising; the inner sign is the firefly appearance. The forty thoughts associated with the transformation of desire cease.
3. Attainment dissolves into clear light. Then, when the consciousness gathers in the middle of the red and white elements, the external sign that arises is pitch black like Rahu; the inner sign is like a butter lamp in a vase. The seven thoughts related to the transformation of ignorance cease.
4. At the time when thoughts dissolve, and when consciousness dissolves into its subtle aspect, the great clear light arises. At that time, the inner sign is for it to be as if there is a sky free from clouds. The mother and son clear lights merge, which is death with liberation, enlightenment in the expanse of the dharmakaya. (At this point, Jamyang Khyentse Wangpo quoted the lines from the *Namasangiti* starting, "Liberation directly on the primordial ground, Samantabhadra. . . .") After that, the union of no-training arises as the sambhogakaya: A multitude of emanations spread out to fill the whole of space, and they accomplish the welfare of sentient beings.

If the person is not liberated at death in the expanse of the dharmakaya, the unity of training arises as bhumi bodhisattvas, and they go to whatever pure celestial realm they wish to go to where they progress on the stages of the path.

Aspiration for clear light is the most important, it is said.

Appearance, flaring, and attainment each have four wisdoms: the wisdom of appearance, the wisdom of flaring, the wisdom of attainment, and the wisdom of full attainment. Empty, greatly empty, extremely empty, and completely empty are the four emptinesses.

In short there are the four visions, the four emptinesses, the four wisdoms, the four clear lights, and so on. [JR]

63. At the time of clear light, you visualize the deity, empty with the channels, wheels, and so on.

> At the time of sleep, meditate evenly on the
> indestructible bindu at the center of the heart. ⁸

The practitioner clearly visualizes a white energy-bindu in the center of a red eight-petaled lotus at the heart. The white energy-bindu then becomes blue, just the size of a mustard seed and with a white A syllable in its middle.

The shallow luminosity is like when you know that you are asleep and have great control over dreaming or not dreaming. It is like when you are resting in the state of undistracted mind luminosity. There are subtle thoughts. The practitioners perceive the sounds, speech, and so on, that are around them; they see, hear, and think.

The deep luminosity: From the moment the practitioner falls asleep until waking up, there is not the slightest double delusion. Even though the practitioners do not know clearly whether they hold the luminosity or not, they rest in the essence the moment they wake up, and that day their elements, subtle essences, and awareness are very clear, through which they realize that they have been holding luminosity in their sleep.

The luminosity of *nyam* experience: The general experiences of bliss, clarity, and the absence of thoughts, and, in particular, due to these experiences of bliss or clarity, luminosity has become constant throughout day and night. In the practitioner's eye, there is a white drop of light or a mark that resembles a tapering brass horn. This provides the right condition for the superknowledges to manifest clearly.

Agitation and experiences like panic in a dream, for example, provide the condition for recognizing the double delusion and recognizing wakeful awareness. This is "the recognition of the agitation."

The luminosity of realization: However many times you stray into distraction and confusion during the day, at night when you hold the clear light, awareness abides directly upon the ground and there is no confused mind.

Shallow luminosity is variable, while deep luminosity is positive, and the luminosity of *nyam* experiences is mostly deceitful; recognizing the agitation is slightly positive, and the luminosity of realization is unchanging. [JR]

64. Capturing dreams means to recognize the double delusion. [JR]

65. To "manifest apparitions" means to make one thing out of several, and to produce many things from a single source—emanating and dissolving, and manifesting whatever is necessary to tame beings, just as manifesting water is the antidote to fire or hawks as the "antidote" to small birds.

"To transform" means to transform fire into water and water into fire.

"To multiply" refers to spreading countless manifestations in the universe.

To develop proficiency is to roam in the whole of samsara and nirvana. In short, at the time of a dream, you are training as if you have complete freedom and control in whatever you do. [JR]

66. Transference: In the lesser transference involving some stages of generation, there are three notions—consider the central channel as the path; thoughts and cognitions as travelers; and the pure fields as a home. [JR]

67. The nine doors from which consciousness may exit the body are (1–2) the two lower doors, the rectum and the urinary tract, (3) the navel, (4) the mouth, (5) the two nostrils, (6) the two eyes, (7) the two ears, (8) the spot between the eyebrows, and (9) the aperture of Brahma. (Here, the aperture of Brahma is not the one at the upper extremity of the central channel).

There is transference into a support or no support. With support, focus on kayas and pure fields; without support, free from reference point, bring together basic space and awareness. [JR]

68. The mental body of the bardo is comprised of the four 'name aggregates', which are the four aggregates of sensations, perceptions, formations, and consciousness; they are the aggregates contained in a mental form. [JR]

69. This is the time to recollect the wisdom of the empowerments that ripen, the development and completion of the paths that liberate, the root and branch samayas that are to be kept, and the qualities of the fruition to be attained.

    *Join together by mixing . . . and the great wisdom.*³ This concludes the section on the secret empowerment, where we have added the special teaching of the sovereign Marpa on mingling and transference. [JR]

70. The notes for the topic of the knowledge-empowerment should be found separately. [JR]

    Tulku Urgyen Rinpoche said that these notes are quite copious and fill a small volume in themselves. He had not seen them outside of Tibet. [EPK]

For information regarding video and audio recordings, published teachings and programs in the lineage of the Chokling Tersar, please access the following websites:

www.lotustreasure.com

www.rangjung.com
Rangjung Yeshe Publications and Translations

www.shedrub.org
Shedrub Development Mandala

www.tsoknyirinpoche.org
Tsoknyi Rinpoche Activities and Teachings

www.CGLF.org
Chokgyur Lingpa Foundation

www.erikpemakunsang.com
Works of Erik Pema Kunsang

www.all-otr.org
Teachings of Orgyen Tobgyal Rinpoche